HOW 'N SYNC ARE YOU WITH YOUR FAVORITE GROUP?

DO YOU KNOW . . .

Lance's favorite TV show and actress?
(*Friends* and Jennifer Aniston)

What JC Collects?
(Hard Rock Café menus)

Joey's favorite author?
(Shakespeare)

What makes Chris blush?
("fine girls")

Justin's musical influences?
(Brian McKnight and Take 6)

'N SYNC

Anna Louise Golden

St. Martin's Paperbacks

'N SYNC

Copyright © 1999 by Anna Louise Golden.

Cover photograph © London Features/Anthony Cutajar.

ISBN: 0-312-97198-2

Printed in the United States of America

St. Martin's Paperbacks edition/April 1999

10 9 8 7 6 5 4 3 2 1

ACKNOWLEDGMENTS

As always, there's no way to begin a book without thanking my brilliant agent, Madeleine Morel. It's hard to believe there could be any better, and I'm certainly not looking! My editor, Glenda Howard, is magic, and I'm glad we're working together again. Friends and family have done their bit, of course. Mum and Dad, L&G, Lee, Greg, people in Seattle and England ... well, you know who you are, and you know you have my undying thanks. Without your love and support, this book would have been a lesser thing, if it had happened at all. And thanks, London, for revitalizing me!

The source material for this book came from articles in *Tiger Beat, 16, Bop, BB, Teen Machine, All Stars, Teen Dream, Frida Poster, Faces In Pop, America Online,* as well as *Rolling Stone* ("'N Sync" by David Wild, November 12, 1998), *Teen People,* November 1998 ("*Getting 'N Sync*" by Lori Majewski), *Teen,* December 1998, and *Billboard* (Wolfgang Spahr, June 21, 1997). If there are any others that have been missed, please contact me and full credit will be given in any future editions.

TABLE OF CONTENTS

INTRODUCTION

Overnight sensations never really happen overnight. Even when someone seems to have sprung from nowhere, there's always a long story to tell. Take 'N Sync: In 1998, they suddenly burst on America as if the whole country had been waiting just for them (it had—it just didn't know it). But before the five hotties enjoyed their success here was a lot of hard work winning fans in Europe, gaining lots of experience. Even that was far from the start of the tale. These were five guys who'd put everything on the line for this band, who'd spent *years* singing, moving, getting it all right, first as individuals, then together. That's a lot of work.

But it's more than paid off. Their 1998 debut album, *'N Sync*, went triple platinum in the U.S.—that's an amazing three million copies sold! They've had two smash hit singles, "I Want You Back" and "Tearin' Up My Heart." The Disney Channel special that really made everyone at home aware of them was one of the highest-rated shows the network had ever had. And, just to make sure they rounded off the year on a high note, they released a Christmas album, *Home For Christmas*, that shot straight into the Top Ten, appeared on television five times in six weeks, and they're playing six months of headlining dates all across the U.S., right after another tour, opening for Janet Jackson. Can a year get any better than that? Quite probably; they're still rising. America has gotten in sync with all the other countries who realize just how great and how cool these guys are, and how in sync with each other their voices sound—the basis for their name.

Justin, JC, Lance (aka Lansten), Chris, and Joey have got it totally going on. They've each spent years learning their craft, putting it all together—and with a little bit of luck to complement all that talent—and now they're getting their rewards. Even their names are in sync with each other—justiN, chriS, joeY, lansteN, jC. What more can anyone ask for?

It all came together in Orlando, Florida, which just also happened to be the home of *the* other American boy band, the Backstreet Boys. But don't go thinking that 'N Sync are a BSB clone. They might have the same manager, Johnny Wright, who also helped New Edition to stardom at the beginning of the Nineties, but 'N Sync are completely their own people. They have their own sound, their own moves, their own style, their own everything. This was something they'd worked toward for a long time, and with their talent, they didn't need to jump on any bandwagons.

It all began in 1995, when Chris Kirkpatrick was earning a living singing Fifties-style doo-wop songs at Universal Studios in Orlando. He met Joey Fatone, who was also a performer there. When the two of them discovered they had some vocal magic happening together, Chris called an old friend, Justin Timberlake, who was also living in Orlando, as part of the cast of *The Mickey Mouse Club*. Someone who was also on the show, and who'd become a friend of Justin's, was JC Chasez. JC and Joey, it turned out, had already known each other for a few years, and Joey also knew Justin. It was as if fate had just been waiting for the four of them to find each other.

"We really put ourselves together," Justin explained. "It's funny to look back on how well we all came together; it just happened step by step."

The four of them worked hard for months. Every night, when they'd finished their jobs, they'd rehearse for four hours. They all knew that they had something good, but they wanted to make it into something perfect. Something was still missing, and they figured out what it was—another voice to take the bass end. Justin called the man who'd been his vocal coach when he lived in Memphis and got a recommendation, the perfectly named James Lance "Lansten" Bass. Lance jumped on a plane down to Florida, and immediately fitted in as if he'd been born for the part. Now there was even more rehearsal. Finally, when they were all satisfied with their harmonies and their sound, they went into the studio and made a demo package—a CD, video, and posters—which they sent out to a number of managers.

One of those people who received a copy of the demo was Lou Pearlman, who remains their business manager. Lou had been involved with the Backstreet Boys, and knew a good thing when he heard it. He called his friend, Johnny Wright, who was in Germany with BSB, just raving about the band.

When Johnny saw them, he agreed. 'N Sync had that special something. They were stars. All they needed was an audience, and getting them that was Johnny Wright's specialty. The first thing they needed was a record deal, and BMG in Germany was on the case in no time, flying the boys over to Europe, where they recorded with Denniz Pop and Max Martin, the team who'd done so well with Ace of Base, Robyn, and . . . the Backstreet Boys. In a few weeks, they'd made their first single, "I Want You Back." And in a few months, that single had already gone gold in Germany. That was followed by "Tearin' Up My Heart," which debuted in the top five.

They weren't just doing well, they were doing phenomenally, breaking all kinds of records all over Europe. At one time Michael Jackson had held the title of fastest-rising single—until 'N Sync came along. Everywhere they turned, they had the Midas touch, turning records into gold and platinum. For two years they toured all over, playing sold-out shows around the globe—everywhere but the United States. But they were in such great demand there was no time to concentrate on the home market.

They conquered Europe, and then turned their attention to Britain, where boy bands had been so popular for years—at least until the Spice Girls and All Saints came along. Take That, East 17, and Boyzone had ruled the charts there for a while. BSB had done phenomenally well there, but when 'N Sync came along, the girls—and the magazines—fell in love with them. They didn't just win the hearts of an island, they also won its charts.

From there, toward the end of 1997, it was on to Asia, South Africa, and Mexico, making a lot of friends and selling a lot of records along the way, until, finally, they could come home. They'd been gone eighteen months, and seen their lives change completely. Throughout Europe things had become so crazy, Justin said, that "We usually have to take two or three bodyguards with us there."

Returning to Florida offered the boys something of a "reality check," Justin admitted. Back home, no one knew they were famous. They could hang out, go where they pleased without being hounded by fans. It gave them exactly the down time they needed to spend with friends and family, to remember what normal life was all about.

But it would only be temporary. The rest of the world had got in sync, and America's turn was coming in 1998. It started early in the new year with a series of magazine interviews and photo shoots, followed by visits to the three major music networks (MTV, VH1, and Much-Music in Canada).

The country was ready to hear them, and their American label, RCA, pulled out all the stops to make sure everyone got the chance. In February, the single and video of "I Want You Back" were released. The single was a smash in every radio format, from Top Forty to dance, and the video was soon in heavy rotation on television.

One thing the band knew how to do was promote the record. The fact that they were now a hit at home meant a lot to all of them. This was *their* country. Their families, the people who knew them and had encouraged them all lived here. To be able to show everyone success was important. And meeting new fans, making new friends, was important, too. After their album, *'N Sync*, appeared on March 24, 1998, the band spent a lot of time on the road, visiting radio stations, signing CDs in record stores, getting close to those who were spending their hard-earned money on their songs.

Early May found them in the Midwest, in the Minneapolis suburb of Bloomington, at the Mall of America, America's biggest mall, playing a free concert for seven thousand screaming fans, more than they'd ever expected to see at home.

Then it was back home to Orlando, and the grand opening of Animal Kingdom at Walt Disney World, a weekend-long event with them as the big attraction, a massive concert that was filmed and would be televised in July on the Disney Channel.

Meanwhile, the album was selling like the proverbial hotcakes. Record stores could hardly keep it in stock, it was so popular. It rocketed onto the charts, and within three months it had gone platinum, with one million satisfied customers. By the end of 1998, that figure would climb to *four* million and still counting. And once *Home for Christmas* was released in November, it immediately joined *'N Sync* in the Top Ten of the *Billboard* album charts.

'N Sync were on a major roll, and they went with it. The summer always brought big concerts hosted by radio stations, and New York's Z100 was going to be one of the biggest. Z-Day had a dream bill—Gloria Estefan, Olivia Newton-John, K-Ci & JoJo, Matchbox 20, Paula Cole, Third Eye Blind, and Mariah Carey—pretty much a who's who of the Top Forty. Added to that lineup, and blowing everyone away, was 'N Sync.

All through the summer and into the fall, they continued to push themselves to the limit. There were mall tours, sponsored by *YM* magazine, a theme park tour in August that took them to all the Six Flags resorts, state fairs, as well as the month of July north of the border, satisfying the demands of Canadian fans who wanted to see the boys live.

It was exhausting, but it was way cool to know that people wanted to hear *them*. They were the hottest thing around, and they appreciated it. They gave their name to a number of causes including SWAT—Students Working Against Tobacco—and Kids to Kids. They understood the importance of giving something back to the people who were supporting them.

Everyone wanted a piece of 'N Sync. *Live! With Regis & Kathie Lee* had them as guests, and so did *The Tonight Show with Jay Leno* and *Miss Teen Pageant USA*. They hit the basketball court for MTV's *Rock 'N' Jock Presents: The Game*. Over the course of the year, they crisscrossed America so much that it seemed as if they knew every road and airport in the U.S.

It was all for the fans, whether in a concert hall, or one-on-one. They could entertain huge crowds, or just make someone's day with impromptu harmonizing on "Happy Birthday."

The bottom line for 'N Sync, when they were pushing

to break through, or even now, when they're megastars all over the world, is singing. They love to sing together, to dance together. And people understand that, they sense the joy that Justin, Chris, Joey, Lance, and JC take in it all. That's one of the reasons "Tearin' Up My Heart" followed "I Want You Back" as a huge American hit in the summer of 1998, followed by "God Must Have Spent a Little More Time on You," one of the most romantic songs of the year (even though it wasn't a single, it was popular enugh in requests to make the *Billboard* singles chart).

By the time they'd finished their promotional tours, it would have been reasonable to think the band needed a break, and they did. But there was no break in sight for them. Next up was the opening slot on Janet Jackson's tour, which introduced them to even more people, and showed that here was a bunch of guys with real soul, who could sing R&B as convincingly as anybody, along with everything else. And when that finished, 'N Sync went straight into their own headlining tour, thirty-four arena dates all over the U.S., that took them all the way to the end of April, 1999—the only break being a chance to make a new album.

They've managed to do it all, and they've made it look so easy. But behind the rapid rise of the boys are all the hours of rehearsal when they were exhausted, driving themselves on and on, the years with vocal coaches and paying their dues. And a belief in their talents, individually and together. They offer a lesson in perseverance, and the rewards it can bring, and the fact that somewhere, somehow, people will appreciate real talent—which is something the boys have a great deal of.

Each of them brings something different to the mix—a love of soul, R&B, country, doo-wop— and they blend it all together to form the whole called 'N Sync. Anyone who thinks they're just another manufactured group rolled off a production line has never really listened to the way their voices work together, their a capella harmonies, the careful co-ordination of their moves. Yes, it helps that they're great to look at, five total babes, but it's not the most important thing. It's what's going on in the music that matters, and 'N Sync have got that all covered, from top to bottom.

More than anything, it's taken faith in themselves to get where they are. When they first began there were plenty of rejections, but they didn't let it faze them. They *knew* they had something special. They were a group, and they were going to make it—as long as they stuck together.

Justin put it best, borrowing an ideal from his old basketball coach.

"You take this finger and try to break it, and you'll be very successful," he told an interviewer. "But you take this fist—all five of these fingers together—and you won't. I guarantee that."

And there's no danger of them not sticking together in the future. They've spent so long together, so much time in each other's company, that they're like family, and a very close, functional family at that. They hang out together during those brief times at home—which seem to be becoming ever briefer—and know each other's families as well as they know their own. They know they can rely on each other, and they'll never let each other down. 'N Sync show why togetherness and harmony (of all kinds) are two of the coolest qualities to have.

THE BOYS

Y ou see them together on the videos and on stage, you hear them all together on record. But it's pretty obvious that the guys in 'N Sync are all very different (all you have to do is really watch the video for "I Want You Back" to get the idea). They're five separate individuals, five pieces of a puzzle that, together, form a whole picture.

Any top band might be more than the sum of its parts, but without just the right parts, the chemistry wouldn't be there. 'N Sync were lucky to find just the right combination, the perfect magic to make it all work; as anyone who's ever sung or played with others in a group, a band, or a chorus knows, it's not easy. You've got to be willing to compromise, and you can't let your own ego run away with you.

The boys of 'N Sync might be on top of the world, in a position to ask for, and receive, almost anything they want, but one thing they've *never* done is let their egos get too big. They've stayed grounded, connected to their families, to each other. They believe in God, and when a fan sent them each bracelets with the letters "WWJD"

(What Would Jesus Do?), they all began to wear them, and still do. It's a constant reminder that there's something bigger out there.

While they're all different, they do share a belief in 'N Sync, and the kind of drive required to make themselves the best in the world. It takes energy to go on long tours, to spend your days traveling, going from plane to coach to stage to hotel in a kind of unreal life, day after day after day, and then, once that's done, and you're exhausted, to go into a recording studio. It's grueling, but it's a life that Chris, Justin, JC, Joey, and Lance wouldn't swap for any other. It's the culmination of a dream, of all the hours spent rehearsing after they'd finished their day jobs.

None of them expected success on this scale, although they might have hoped for it in their hearts. The fact that it hasn't changed them is a testament to the kind of upbringing each of them had. Without those sets of relatives, old friends, influences, and education, there wouldn't be an 'N Sync. And it certainly doesn't hurt that each of them is cute, either. . . .

CHRIS

Chris is the clown," said Joey.
"Chris is psycho," Justin agreed.
"Chris is wild," Lance admitted.

Everyone in the band is pretty much in agreement about Chris's personality. He's the joker in the pack, the one who likes to laugh, and make everyone else laugh—which he seems to do quite successfully. But without Chris, there might never have been an 'N Sync at all.

He was the one who first had the idea for the band, and who began putting everyone together; he was the initial driving force, and as the oldest, some of that kind of responsibility still falls on his shoulders.

He's the major extrovert in a crew who are all pretty outgoing. He likes things to keep changing, to keep moving. The one thing he really can't stand is for things to be static.

"I'm the most hyper member of the group," he admitted. "I need lots of calming down." Press him, and he will say that "I have a really short attention span, so things tend to bore me easily."

And that's the main reason he changes his appearance

so often. Over the course of just over twelve months he went from short hair to wearing a pageboy, to long and dyed black, to the cornrow-type dreadlocks he currently wears. And his hair can change color on a whim, too. Well, why *not*?

Christopher Alan Kirkpatrick was born in Clarion, Pennsylvania, on October 17, 1971. Clarion, not far from Pittsburgh at the western end of the state, was a small town, a comfortable place for a young boy. He was the first child for Beverly and her husband, a man who'd tragically die when Chris was still young.

There were two things in Chris's blood—Pennsylvania and music. Beverly's family was from the area, and most of her relatives had been involved with music in one way or another. Her grandparents had been in bands, her mother had trained as an opera singer, her sister still sings professionally, and both Chris's uncles were singers, one in a rock band, the other in Nashville, trying his hand at country. Even Chris's cousin sang. Beverly herself played piano and gave—still gives, in fact—voice lessons as a vocal coach.

So it was perhaps inevitable that Chris would inherit the family talent for music, as well as the love of Pennsylvania. He's still a football fan, having come from an area where the gridiron is king, and supports the Pittsburgh Steelers and the Penn State Nittany Lions. But when he was a baby, he said, Bev never gave him a pacifier. Instead he had a small football to suck on. He played the game for a few years, in junior high and high school, even though he was small for his age, but he was never good enough to think of pursuing it seriously.

Besides, his real gift was music. It was all around the house from the time he was born.

"I know that when I was born I pretty much was singing," he remembered. "My mom said I could sing before I could talk. I just know that I've always loved music and loved listening to music and performing."

In fact, he *literally* was singing before he could talk. Beverly used to sing to him at night to help him sleep, and usually it was "Coventry Carol," an old hymn, that sent him to sleep. She was astonished one day, when, before he could even make words, he was singing the tune back to her.

It wasn't just tunes; Chris had been born with a great sense of rhythm. As a toddler, whenever music came on the television, he'd tap his foot in time with the beat. There was no doubt about it; music was a huge part of him.

Just how huge was apparent even before he was three. His mother had gone to see the musical *Man of La Mancha*, and had taken Chris along with her as a treat. She'd expected he'd enjoy it. What she hadn't expected was that Chris would memorize two of the songs from just hearing them one time.

Even back then, Chris was a real ham. He loved to perform, even demanded to perform once at a family reunion. After everyone else, the grown-ups and the older children, had done their party pieces, he jumped onto a table, said, "Hey, what about me!" and began to sing for everybody.

After the death of her husband, Beverly remarried and would eventually give birth to three more children, giving Chris four younger half-sisters, Molly, Kate, Emily, and Taylor. The new family moved to Dayton, Ohio, which was where Chris attended school.

Dayton, some forty miles north of Cincinnati, was probably most famous for being the home of Wright Air Force base. It still had something of a small-town feel about it, so, while it was quite a bit bigger than Clarion, Chris didn't feel uncomfortable there. He settled into the routine of school. When Michael Jackson hit really big in the early 1980s with *Thriller* and a great series of singles, he became Chris's musical idol—reasonable, because not only was Jackson having massive success, he was doing something *new*.

As he grew, not only did Chris get into sports, but he continued his interest in music. He began studying guitar and piano. The piano lessons didn't last too long, however. Chris was simply too hyper to comfortably sit still on a piano stool, and finally his teacher had to let him go from class.

His singing voice came quite naturally, and he nurtured it in school stage productions like *Oliver!* and *South Pacific*. His moment of revelation, figuring out just how much he really enjoyed entertaining people, came after he won the lead in the school production of *Oliver!* It gave him the chance to really express himself in song and dance, and also to hear the applause, the feedback of an audience. He also began to get a reputation as the class clown, which, his mother suspected, was something of a defense mechanism, because he was so small: If he could entertain the other kids, they wouldn't beat him up.

It was probably necessary. Not only was Chris small, he was also a gifted student, outstanding not only in music (big surprise, right?) but also languages, and very strong academically in all his other subjects. He worked hard at school, and enjoyed it, both the work he had to do and the extracurricular activities.

One thing he needed, even then, was to have all the moments of his day filled, and Chris found that it was the time *after* school and on the weekends that seemed to drag. So he remedied that situation by finding himself a job, bagging groceries in a local market. He was, his mother said, "hardworking," and that was an ethic that would stand him in good stead in the time to come.

At school, Chris was active in the choir, and also in various theater productions. They gave him a chance to step into the spotlight, to channel all his energy into something constructive. He could be the clown, the star, whatever, and it was okay; in fact, it was an area where people applauded him for doing that. Given the chance, he would always show his goofy side. In one high school production of *South Pacific*, his character died. When Chris came out at the end, to take his bow—this for a performance that had had people crying because of its sensitivity—he was dressed in a grass skirt and coconut shell bra. Nothing was sacred to him.

Perhaps not *nothing*. He was very serious about music. It seemed to hold a fascination for him over and above everything else, the family genes asserting themselves. Beverly made sure he had voice lessons so he could use his talent properly. Those gave him a grounding in all kinds of music, from opera to the Beatles, and helped him expand his range into the falsetto he can still use on stage and on record with 'N Sync.

Being bright, it was inevitable that Chris would go on to college to complete his education, but he didn't choose the obvious route of university. Instead, he went to Valencia College, in Dayton, where he picked his Associate of Arts degree, "and then I transferred to Rollins College," in Florida.

At Valencia, Chris had begun by majoring in theater, but he quickly realized that wasn't what he wanted to do with his life. He loved being in front of an audience, but it was the musical side of things that really affected him, more than learning lines and being part of a play.

Another of his interests was psychology, getting inside the human mind, and understanding what makes people tick, trying to help those with problems. Chris changed his major from theater to music and psychology, and for a brief while even considered combining the two, to become a music therapist, using his love to help those with problems.

College did give him more time to indulge his love of music. He joined the college choir, and performed, solo—remember, he could play guitar and piano—and with groups in coffeehouses around Dayton to earn a little extra cash.

His two years at Valencia went smoothly, and Chris walked away with his degree. The question was what would he do now. More college seemed like the best answer. But, at twenty years old, he was ready to spread his wings a little, to move out of his mother's home and see the world a little. The obvious answer seemed to be Florida, where his ex-stepfather was living. That would give him freedom, but still enough of a safety net, if anything should ever go wrong. Florida was also a good place to be to pursue the acting side of his interests. Universal Studios was there. So was Disney, and Nickelodeon. In fact, there was a whole industry down there. To be an actor you didn't need to go to New York or Los Angeles anymore.

One thing Chris would need to help him through the two years of academic work he still had to get his B.A. was money. Acting didn't seem like a safe answer; there was never any guarantee of steady work, unless you happened to be very lucky. The coffeehouse work in Dayton had shown him that he could earn with his music, but he needed more than just tips to survive now that he was living on his own, with rent and bills to pay.

The answer came from Universal Studios. The studio tour was an immensely popular attraction, and there was entertainment all over the site. They were constantly looking for good performers, and Chris knew that with his ability and extroverted personality, he could fit in there. But it didn't happen straight away. His first Christmas in Florida, Chris sang with a group called the Caroling Company, which proved to be very good money for what amounted to a couple of days' work. Others in the group were working at Universal and helped Chris get an audition—which he naturally passed with flying colors.

"I used to sing with a Fifties doo-wop group called

the Hollywood High Tones," he recalled. "We used to sing outside the Fifties diner at Universal. That was me—it was three guys and one girl and we'd sing Fifties a capella music. My name was Spike, but my hair was a little different then."

Quite a lot different, really, greased back in a pompadour, shiny and stiff, and "Spike" was dressed in period clothes—short-sleeve shirts and cuffed jeans. Maybe it wasn't the music Chris had in his heart, but it was a living.

Chris wasn't taking a full courseload at Rollins; that was impossible when he was also working full-time at Universal. But it was fine. Slowly, gradually, he was working toward his degree. However, deep inside, he was beginning to realize that it was music he loved above everything else, and that was where he should be putting his energies. And for him, vocal music was the inspiration. The Beatles, Simon and Garfunkel, Michael Jackson, and Boyz II Men were the ones who moved him. He had his own vision of a group where the vocals were the most important things, some guys with great voices all blending together.

But it wasn't until a co-worker introduced him to Joey Fatone, who was also performing at Universal, that Chris seriously began thinking about making his dream a reality. They sang together, and it sounded better than they could have imagined. But it was only when Chris called Justin, whom he'd met at auditions, and Justin brought in JC that things began to happen. Actually, Joey didn't even know there *was* a band until he ran into Chris and JC in a club one night. They asked him to join, and before they knew it, they were a real band.

Between work, rehearsals, and studies, Chris was stretched to the limit. Something would have to give, and for Chris, it had to be college.

"They kicked me out of class to do the group," was his joke. "No, they didn't really kick me out. I had to drop out of Rollins to do the group. I didn't have time to do college and the group.'' Chris, it seemed, had found his vocation in life.

For the first time, Chris was really taking music seriously. With the other guys—especially after Lance arrived to anchor the bass end—he sensed the possibilities. When he called Beverly to tell her his reason for dropping out of school, she wasn't upset, or even too surprised. She'd always known, even more than he did, that Chris had the music in him. All she wanted, for any of her children, was for them to be happy, and if this would bring Chris some joy, she encouraged him to go for it. If it all worked out and made him rich, that would be wonderful. But it was more important that it left him fulfilled. And it quickly became apparent that the newly-named 'N Sync was going to do that. She couldn't have anticipated what was going to happen . . . no one could.

Of course, from putting the band together to international stardom took a lot of work and dedication, but the end result has been more than worth all the time and effort. And, for Chris, it's a dream come true. The original idea might have been Chris's, but, as he said, ''I know how hard [the others] work and their reasons for doing it, I just think they're incredible.'' So incredible, in fact, that they've become his biggest musical influence now. When he was asked the secret of his success in an online interview, he gave the short, truthful answer: ''Justin, JC, Lance, Joey.''

But he certainly doesn't forget the role that 'N Sync's fans have played in their rise; he knows they're at the heart of it all, and that they make it all worthwhile.

Chris's life might have changed beyond all recognition from the young man who was singing doo-wop and going to school in Florida, but he hasn't changed at all. According to his mother, who remains the biggest role model in his life (along with Jesus), Chris is exactly the same person he's always been—which means wild, crazy, and often hyper.

So it's no surprise that when he has the time, he engages in a lot of physical activities. He plays basketball, shooting hoops for hours, often with other guys from the band, and in-line skates. And then there's the sun and sand of Florida.

"I like beaches and I live near one," he said, and he takes advantage of the water, too, going surfing, whatever the weather—including one time in heavy wind and rain that was almost a hurricane!

Being so energetic makes life on the road, with its interminable traveling and waiting, difficult for Chris, but he's gradually learned to cope with it. "We've got crazy hours," he admitted, "but I've learned to sleep on airplanes a lot and in vans."

Catching sleep wherever and whenever they can has become a normal part of life for all the guys of 'N Sync. All too often, when on tour or making a series of promotional appearances, their meals are grabbed on the run, which means a lot of fast food—handy for Chris, since he loves pizza and tacos more than anything. Sometimes the fans can get out of hand, but for the most part they've been amazingly polite.

Their schedules have been so busy that downtime has become a valuable commodity for the guys. Chris had lived apart from his family even before the band started, but that doesn't means he's missed them any less. Given the chance, he retreats to his mom's, where he can play with his littlest sister, Taylor, and his three nephews. Occasionally, Beverly will travel with Chris, and she spent some time in Acapulco when the band was performing there, but that chance doesn't come too often, since she still works full-time, gives voice lessons, and also looks after her grandkids—as full a schedule as Chris! Even when he's gone, though, the two of them will talk regularly on the phone, and Chris will ask his mother for her advice and opinion—which he always gets.

These days, Chris's home—well, Beverly's home—has become something of a tourist attraction, with buses circling the block, and girls ringing the doorbell. While she's been happy to talk to them, at times it's become difficult for all his family. At school, kids would come up to Chris's sister, Emily, to the point where she's ended up home-schooling to avoid all the hassle. And Beverly herself has had fans visit her and call her at work.

One thing that happened when 'N Sync hit big was that they acquired a whole bunch of new ''friends''—hangers-on, basically, who wanted the guys for what they could get out of them, posing as fans. One advantage of Chris's age and maturity is that he's known these people weren't real, and he's been able to get rid of them.

But real is a very important word to Chris. He keeps everything real—the music, the world, and most particularly his own life. With the way everything's gone, it would have been understandable if his feet had left the ground for a while, but he's kept them firmly planted on the earth. He still works hard, and plays hard. And when he does want quiet times by himself at home, there's his Sony PlayStation, and the chance to play music, or catch up with episodes of his favorite show, *South Park*, just for the enjoyment of it.

More recently, he also discovered writing. ''I love writing and listening to music so I've invested in a laptop [computer] to make life easier,'' he said. Now he can take his own world on the road with him, anywhere in the world.

And he remains the band cut-up.

''Chris is probably the funniest,'' JC said. ''I think everybody has their moments, but Chris just seems to have more of them.'' He's funny, and he's *fast*, quick off the mark with a joke or a remark to get everyone laughing.

Apart from making sure he doesn't have much of a

home life, the frantic schedule of 'N Sync hasn't done much for Chris's chance of romance, either. There simply hasn't been the time for him to really get to know anyone properly, in depth. While there are girls he'll go out with, there's no real girlfriend. As he puts it, "I'm twenty-seven years old; I'm allowed to date!" Not that he doesn't have a vision of an ideal girl, with a lovely smile, one he can get so close to that they'll complete each other's sentences. He'll find her, of course, but it might be later rather than sooner, as the band goes from strength to strength all around the globe.

If one word can sum up Chris, it's probably casual. He can manage to be constantly moving and laid-back all at the same time. And that's reflected in the way he dresses, which is kind of funky, but also sporty, ready for any kind of action. You can usually find him in baggy jeans or skater pants, and oversized team jerseys, from any sort of sport. And then, of course, there are the sunglasses that he seems to have around all the time, sometimes with dark lenses, sometimes bright yellow. Onstage, in the videos, almost everywhere, he has a pair handy.

One thing that's slightly less obvious is the tattoo that Chris has. It's on the back of his calf, usually hidden by his pants leg. The design is the image that adorns the actual disk of *'N Sync*, put in his skin more elaborately, in several colors. So far he's the only member of the band to sport a tattoo, and it was something he chose because the graphic, just like the music, represents a great deal to him. Did it hurt? He's never said, but he's certainly proud of it.

For now, Chris is thoroughly content with his life. He's doing something he loves, with four other guys who are as close to him as brothers. He's up on stage, entertaining huge crowds, singing and dancing, fulfilling the dream that began all those years ago with *Oliver!* But he also loves being in the studio, and having the chance to perfect their sound. When they're home in Florida, the guys continue to rehearse on a regular basis, refining their moves, their harmonies, and working on new material. The fact that the band has been writing is exciting to him. Chris and Justin have come up with a couple of raps, and one of his proudest moments has been the inclusion of the song "Giddy Up," which was co-written by the group, on the 'N Sync album. It's a sign of what's to come, as they exercise their creativity more and more. For himself, Chris has some musical ambitions outside the group; someday he'd love to work with Busta Rhymes or Missy Elliott. The way things keep going, that might well happen in the future.

But that's way ahead. For now he's completely happy with the way things are going, and the chance to be "the crazy one, the loud one, the Psycho Spice." Nor does he feel any sense of competition with the Backstreet Boys, most of whom are close to his age. To Chris, both bands have something very positive to offer everyone. They both entertain, and both try to inspire. They may be wholesome—in BSB it's AJ who comes closest to Chris's wild image—but they're very human, real people. Both bands are made up of individuals who are together because they *want* to be, because they work, live, and sing well together.

'N Sync is Chris's baby. It was his idea, and he's nurtured it along, with plenty of help from a lot of people. He's earned the right to be incredibly proud of what they've achieved. Selling more than four million albums in America, having two albums in the *Billboard* Top Ten at the same time—these are things that very few have achieved. The same goes for the success they've enjoyed overseas.

A side of Chris that fewer see is his sensitivity. He's very aware that a lot of people haven't been as fortunate as him, and he's always willing to try and find the time to be able to give something back to people who've supported him, and who haven't been as successful. When he was a kid, he once gave away a lot of his family's groceries to another family that had nothing. These days, he—and the rest of the band—take part in charity shows to raise money.

"I think you just do as much as you can," is his opinion. "When I was little, I tried to do as much as I could as often as I could. Now that we've got a name out there, it's a lot easier for us to do more for charity because you can appeal to the masses." He'll event stretch his schedule tighter to take part in a worthwhile event. "[W]hen it's for a good cause and the crowd gets you hyped up it always makes it so much easier," he said.

His life might have gone through a lot of changes, but his heart is quite firm and secure in the right place. The vision he had has become reality, and life has become everything he could ever have imagined, and more. The fact that 'N Sync came together of its own accord—not the manufactured group some critics think they are—is important to him. It's all about integrity, about doing it right, and being honest, the values that are uppermost in his life. With his talent and his foresight, Chris is going to be around in music for a long time to come. Having risen, his star isn't going to fade anytime soon. If anything, it'll just get higher and higher—right along with the rest of the band. They're riding the wave, and there's no end in sight. But when you're this good, why should there be? Everyone has years of albums and shows to look forward to yet, and that can only be good news.

JOEY

He's the talker of the band, the tall one (just about six feet) with the brown hair, brown eyes, the open, smiling face, and the goatee. At twenty-three, he's the middle one in the band, age-wise, and he's probably the one who looks at everything 'N Sync the most objectively. He thinks and weighs his ideas, then takes off speaking at a mile a minute, like the New Yorker he once was.

"Joey definitely talks the most," Chris agrees. "Once he starts, he just goes rambling on and he doesn't stop for breath. It all ends up being one huge, long sentence, like this, and you find yourself trying to breathe for him!"

Like Chris, he's always had music inside him, just waiting to come out and be heard. But more than anyone else in the band, he's the entertainer, the one who loves putting on a full show. He trained in dance, worked as an entertainer. What he's doing with the other guys is just what he was put on this earth to do—make people happy, even the other boys in 'N Sync.

"I cheer the guys up when they get down," he said,

and if the group had a cheerleader, it would be Joey. It all began as Chris's idea, but Joey was there right at the beginning, too. It all means so much to him.

Joey was born Joseph Anthony Fatone, Junior, in the Bensonhurst section of Brooklyn, New York, on January 28, 1977. His parents, Joe, Sr., and Phyllis, already had two children, Janine, five years older than Joey, and Steven, two years older. The Fatones were a Catholic, Italian-American family, and that meant lots of visits to church, and a large extended family in the neighborhood—real old-school Brooklynites.

There was plenty of love and attention around for the kids, relatives their own age they could go and play with after school, and all the holidays, especially Christmas, turned into major celebrations. Joey, though, usually arrived with some kind of injury. Until he was five years old, he seemed like the most accident-prone kid in America, always on his way to the emergency room following a fall or a tumble—in large part because he'd try and imitate his first hero, Superman. Unfortunately, Joey had yet to realize he wasn't the Man of Steel, and so there'd be cuts requiring stitches, which would end up in scars that he still carries all over his body. The fascination with Superman never did vanish, however; even now, Joey still collects all manner of Superman memorabilia.

Music entered Joey in his genes. His father was a singer, and music was just naturally around the house, songs from the Fifties and Sixties on the record player, and also sung by Joe, Sr., who was a singer in a doo-wop group.

"He used to sing in a group called the Orions," Joey remembered. "They weren't famous, but they were great. They had records and stuff and every time they played, I would be singing and stuff like that behind my dad."

The Orions did indeed release a couple of records, which sold to relatives, friends, and fans around Brooklyn, but never got them anywhere near the big time. And in the early Eighties, not too many people were buying doo-wop records, anyway. The Orions did what they did for sheer fun. They used to practice at the Fatone house, and Joey, Janine, and Steven just used to watch them in awe as they rehearsed.

That early exposure to pure singing—the Orions were purely vocal, with no instruments behind the voices—was undoubtedly a big influence on Joey, and it was cemented as he grew and his father played him records by bands that really influenced the vocals, from all the eras of pop music, like Frankie Lymon and the Teenagers, Boyz II Men, and the Motown groups like the Temptations and the Four Tops. He received a strong grounding in music.

But it was more than just knowledge that stirred him. Joey loved to sing, too, and as soon as he could, that was what he was doing around the house, performing for his family, the first complete song being the oldie, "Tequila," for which he even worked out a dance routine!

That was his very first performance, but many others would quickly follow. The Fatones were associated with a few churches in their Brooklyn neighborhood, and they all put on plays and musicals. So, from an early age Joey, his brother, and his sister, found themselves treading the boards. Joey's first exposure to an audience beyond his family came in *Oklahoma!*, and his first real speaking part was in *Pinocchio*, when he was still in kindergarten. He only had a small role, but it left an indelible impression on him, hearing the applause of an audience just for him. Even though he was young, he realized that he loved the feeling it gave him, and he wanted more.

He got more, too—carrying on acting in church plays, singing, even doing some dancing, all the way through grade school. It lasted until he was thirteen, and his parents decided to finally leave Brooklyn and move down to the sunshine of Florida.

"Growing up, every time there was a vacation, we'd

come down to Florida," he explained. "When a certain [Brooklyn] neighborhood and the area was getting a bit bad, my family wanted to move to Florida. It's sunny all the time and nice. The houses were a little bit cheaper and there was actually more space."

They decided to settle in Orlando. For all of them, it was a big move, not just in terms of distance, but also leaving behind the network of friends and family that had grown over several generations. But it gave more opportunity to Joe, Sr., and, more importantly, to the kids, even if they didn't see it that way at first. All of a sudden, they were the new kids in school.

For Joey, the best way to adjust to his new surroundings and make friends was to get involved in plays and shows. High school meant more musicals than dramas, and with his voice, he was eager to be part of those. However, he couldn't dance, at least not in any trained way, so "that's when I pretty much got involved with dancing," he said. "I took a little bit of jazz, a little ballet, I *tried* to do tap but . . ."

That was only part of the story. Joey was doing more and more acting outside school, including some Shakespeare, and even landed roles as an extra in a movie filmed in the area, *Matinee* (1992), as well as a brief appearance in the television series *SeaQuest*. But those weren't the first credits on his resume. When he was only seven years old, he'd appeared as an extra in *Once Upon a Time in America* (1984), which had been filmed, in part anyway, in Brooklyn.

Films and television were one avenue that Joey could use to express himself, particularly with the industry that seemed to be sprouting around Orlando. But it was performing onstage that was his real love, and in particular singing. High school gave him the opportunity to explore some of those possibilities, both in productions, and also in the a capella band he formed, following in his father's footsteps—although the music was updated somewhat.

Graduation came around in 1995. It was a big time for Joey, as it is for everyone, both an end and a new beginning. It also meant he had to do some serious thinking about the future. College was a possibility, but he knew in his heart that what he wanted to do was perform and entertain. Four more years of school wouldn't help with that at all. He needed to be *doing* rather than studying. As he walked up to receive his diploma, the applause ringing, he knew he had to do what was best for himself.

"My best moment was graduating high school," he recalled. "It was great. It was sad, but it was happy because everybody that I grew up with over the four years was going off to college and everything to start a career, and this ['N Sync] is what we started and I've been happy ever since."

Of course, the band didn't start immediately. While his friends packed their bags and went off to college, Joey stayed home and went to work, landing a job at the Universal Studios tour. Both his brother and sister were already working there, which helped when he began. But for an eighteen-year-old with a yen for entertaining people, it was the perfect gig. He could be as extroverted as he wanted to be, as loud, and as happy. He was singing and dancing, and being paid for it—as close to an ideal world as he could imagine.

"At Universal, I did a show called *The Beetlejuice Graveyard Review* and I played characters like the Wolfman and Dracula," he explained in *16*. "We did entertainment. As far as that goes, entertainment is entertainment. It's always performing on stage or performing in front of an audience, and that's what we're doing and that's what we love doing."

The costumes were hot during the Florida summer, but Joey really didn't care. He was having the time of his life. He didn't know how much and how quickly his life would change when he met another employee at the park, Chris Kirkpatrick.

Putting a group together might have been Chris's brainchild, but it was Joey, the local boy—well, he'd been local for a few years, anyway—who helped the pieces all fall into place. One of the first friends he'd made after arriving in Florida was Joshua Scott Chasez, known to all his friends as JC. JC was a regular on the Disney Channel show *The Mickey Mouse Club*, and Joey knew most of the cast, since several of them went to his high school. He'd also met another singer and performer who was a few years younger, but who was also on *The Mickey Mouse Club*, a boy called Justin Timberlake, who'd become a good friend of JC's. So when Joey ran into Chris and JC and heard about this new band, he already knew the guys, and realized he'd be a good fit.

The whole grunge thing had been and gone, and there was something of a void in pop music, although groups like Boyz II Men did offer some inspiration, a realization that pop music could make a return.

Success has been everything Joey ever imagined it would be. As the self-professed "womanizer" and "playboy" of the group, he's never short of a date. But don't worry, it's all innocent. Like all the others, the one thing fame and fortune has taken away from him is time. There's no chance for more than the occasional casual date, no opportunity to really get to know a girl properly. He doesn't really have a "type"—he just likes girls, and in due course he'll undoubtedly find that special one. But she'd better be very tolerant, because, since he was five years old, Joey has been an incorrigible flirt. What he enjoys, and what he does get, is the company of girls—usually several thousand at a time, when 'N Sync is playing a show.

All the guys appreciate their fans, obviously—they all know that without people coming to their concerts and buying their records they'd be nothing—but Joey seems to take an extra special delight in them. He's the one who'll spend those extra few minutes outside the bus, the hotel, or the show to sign autographs and chat with the fans.

"It is pretty flattering, actually, when people say, 'Oh you're that person in 'N Sync. I know who you are.'" The fact that so many people know his face, with its dark brown, slightly unruly hair, goatee, and sideburns, is perhaps inevitable. Along with the other guys, he might well be one of the most recognized people in the world. Some would let that go to their heads, but not these boys. Joey's splashed out and bought himself a new Honda Acura SLX, but that's about as extravagant as he's been. He's polite and charming (not to mention talkative) with everyone he meets; he doesn't put on airs.

"We're still normal guys," he explained. "It's always fun being recognized and everything, which is wonderful, but we're just normal guys. We keep each other in check, and make sure our feet are always on the ground. What you see is what you get."

Success has been wonderful for everyone in the band, but it does have its drawbacks. For Joey, the biggest one is that he doesn't see his family anywhere near as much as he used to do. He's always on the road or in the studio. By now he's learned to deal with any homesickness, but he still loves to take his family on the road when the chance occurs. So far they've been all around the U.S. with him, into Canada, Mexico, and to most of Europe.

Joe, Sr., and Phyllis Fatone have always supported Joey's decision to be an entertainer, even before it began to pay off in a very big way. Joe, Sr., understands what it's like to have that *need* to sing and dance and perform. He encouraged it in all his children. And, as 'N Sync have gotten bigger and bigger, the Fatones have remained involved. Phyllis answered all the fan mail when they were still just a European sensation, and she (along with Joe) still takes care of that, even though the mail has now grown out of all proportion! They use an office next to the Trans Continental studios in Orlando. When he's off on tour or making promotional appearances, Joey stays in regular touch with his parents. Every day they talk at least twice. That means he has some pretty extravagant phone bills, but it's one of the few luxuries in which he indulges—and one which his mom is happy about, even if she does get on his case every month about his phone bills. Joe offers his son financial advice—when he asks for it. Joey is an adult now, and able to make his own decisions.

One decision he hasn't made is about moving out of his parents' house. At the moment Joey has so little free time to spend in Florida that it barely seems worthwhile to have a place of his own, although that will undoubtedly change as time passes. When he is home, however, the same rules apply as when he was younger—his mom still gets on to him to pick up after himself and to make his bed. Perhaps the biggest change is that the Fatones have had to install more closets to accommodate all Joey's clothes. There are plenty he receives from companies, including pairs and pairs of sneakers, hoping he'll wear them and advertise their products, but the majority arrive as gifts from fans, including sweaters—one fan even sent him a hand-knitted sweater that was a reproduction of Superman's jersey.

Yes, Joey still has his Superman fixation. These days, of course, he can afford to buy the more expensive memorabilia, the rare stuff that only collectors can afford, but he doesn't limit himself to that. He has Superman T-shirts, and even wears a medallion with the *S* logo. But at least he's not knotting a dish towel around his neck and hurting himself anymore; these days Joey restricts his flying to airplanes, which is good news for everybody.

Like all the other guys, his house has become a tourist attraction. Phyllis is always happy to talk to them, and if they arrive on one of the rare occasions when Joey's actually at home, he'll come out and spend time with them, have his picture taken, and sign autographs.

It used to be only European fans who'd make the pilgrimage to the Fatone house, but more and more Americans have begun making the trip as 'N Sync have become huge here. And their massive popularity at home has caused a few problems for Joey. When they were only known overseas, he could still have some anonymity in Florida. He could go out and do regular things—run to the store, catch a movie. These days that's harder and harder without his being mobbed by fans.

One place he can get away from it all, however, is in a club.

"I love dancing and going to clubs," he admitted, and when he's out for the night, techno is his music of choice. The pumping beats and the lights in a club just keep him moving until it's almost daylight. But he's earned his chance to relax and work off some steam. 'N Sync have worked incredibly hard for the last few years to reach the position they now occupy. He likes to have fun, and clubbing offers him the kind of physical release that performing does, but away from the audience. He clubbing buddy is usually Chris, and they hit the hot spots together. "Sometimes me and Chris want to go out and party all night," he said.

Sport, too, could offer some release, but Joey is the first to acknowledge that "apart from skating, I'm useless at sports." He did however, enjoy jet-skiing the one time he had the chance to try it, when the band was doing a photo shoot, and when he has the time, he'll probably take more time with that—and living in Florida, there are plenty of places he can jet-ski!

Joey might relish his time at home surrounded by his family, but of the boys, he's the one who *really* enjoys being on the road. For him, the best thing of it is "the travel, definitely. I love visiting different places, London is great. There's a real buzz about the city." But it's not just London, it's everywhere they've been. In every country, Joey's found something to rave about, and he's learned to enjoy the differences. And every place he goes, something you'll find in his carry-on baggage is his camcorder. He loves to document his travels, to be able to watch them later and relive the cities and countries that he's seen. By now, of course, he's accumulated footage from all around the globe; but that's something most guys his age haven't had the chance to do. Joey's been given the opportunity to learn a lot.

Learning is something that fascinates him. He might not have gone on to college, but that doesn't mean his brain quit working after high school. He's learning all the time, in every situation, whether it's in the studio, on a video or a photo shoot, even onstage. And the knowledge he gains he can apply, and keep applying, both in terms of the band, and for himself. Joey's become more than just an entertainer, although that's at the heart of everything he does. He's figured out how to harness his creative side.

Right now, 'N Sync are on top of the world. They have fans all over, and their records sell in the millions. He knows full well that they're not Backstreet Boys copyists. There might be a few superficial similarities (they both have five cute members, and have shared the same management, although BSB are now leaving), but, he notes, 'N Sync have "more intricate harmonies."

It probably comes as no surprise to anyone that Joey loves Italian food; after all, it's in his blood to sit down with a big bowl of pasta and sauce, and he's been doing it since he was a little kid. He prefers it over all the burgers and pizza, and with good Italian restaurants all over the world, he's in luck when the boys are on the road.

Far more than the others, even more than Chris, Joey is the wild dresser of the group. He might look pretty well-groomed, with his hair short, and his goatee neat, but he has a serious wardrobe, including many, many pairs of baggy jeans.

"I've got one pair with fiber optics down the side and they light up," he boasted.

"He does have a style, but it's out there," according to Chris. "He's got crazy stuff! He's got one coat that looks like he killed Chewbacca and one red suit that makes him look like Elmo. And his jeans are humongous!"

That's just a sampling of what he likes to wear. Not when he's performing with the band, of course, but catch him when he's on his own time (a pretty hard thing to do, admittedly) and you'll find him in some of the funkiest threads you've ever seen. It's about the only way he gets outrageous, really, his chance to escape and be totally himself. And if you *do* see him, there's a good chance he'll be wearing something purple, since that's his favorite color

Apart from his family, Joey is close to all the other guys in the band. They've become their own little clique, having experienced all the same things as the group has grown. Success might have happened "so quickly, it still hasn't hit us yet," but they've coped with it very well, in large part because they won't let each other get swelled heads. Being the biggest band in the world is amazing, but if they were to ever believe the hype then that would be the start of the end.

Inevitably, one or other of the guys will feel down from time to time, and that's when Joey's real character shines through. He's a great believer in never giving in to adversity, at working on problems and solving them.

"Joey's a very optimistic person," Justin said. "Whenever things aren't going too good, he'll try his hardest to make them better."

So when someone is low, he takes it on himself to cheer them up, to get things moving along and back to normal. "I cheer the guys up when they get down," he said, adding, "I'm outgoing and try to make people laugh." The guys have so many demands on their time, all the time. There are barely enough hours in the day to eat and sleep, along with all the other appointments. They *have* to stay on top of things. And they have to keep laughing.

Joey can see a time when it all becomes a little less frantic, and when 'N Sync can experiment a bit more. Through his dad he's come to love a wide range of music, and he'd like to see the band working with performers from other musical areas—he's already singled out Janet Jackson and Jewel as people he'd enjoy working with. And why not? If BSB can do a duet with Tony Bennett, then 'N Sync could fit their harmonies into a Janet Jackson song or a Jewel ballad, adding a lot of texture to the material—and bringing in whole new audiences. Given the fact that they've toured with Janet, that kind of collaboration might not be as odd as some people would imagine. Whether this might means there's a Jewel/ 'N Sync double concert bill happening sometime in the future, though, remains to be seen.

Like most people, Joey has a lot of different sides to his personality. While he's often silly and happy, still comfortable with the child inside himself (his all-time favorite movie is *Willie Wonka and the Chocolate Factory* and his best childhood memory is "going to Disney World for the first time"), he can also be quite serious (and obviously kind of nervous, too, since his major bad habit is biting his nails). This is a guy whose favorite book is the Shakespeare play, *Macbeth* (the name of which you're not allowed to utter in a theater—it's bad luck; it has to be referred to as "The Scottish Play"), and whose favorite actor is Robert De Niro, who's not exactly known for his light roles!

Like most of the other guys, however, Joey relaxes in front of the television, in particular with *South Park*. The videos for the shows are a necessity on the 'N Sync tour

buses, along with Nintendo64 and Sony PlayStation—
things to help them pass the hours and the miles on the
road. For Joey, who's more laid-back than Chris, the
boredom of a tour is easier to take. Apart from having
his video camera to document it all, he's learned how to
sleep almost anywhere—just as well since sleep has become something of a luxury in his business.

Also like the others, he's had to learn that not everyone who's nice to him is a fan and genuine. There are
plenty of phonies out there, wanting to buddy up to members of the band for their own end—usually money. Joey,
with that kind of innate sense that New Yorkers seem
born with, can smell them coming a mile away, and he
has no time for them. "The thing I hate most of all is
fake people," he said, and it's quite easy to believe. Who
doesn't? But by the nature of his success, Joey seems
more aware of them than most, and he's learned to tune
his radar very finely. The *real* fans are fine—get Joey
among them and he won't shut up for *hours*. But someone he has his doubts about? He won't even open his
mouth.

It's sad that the world has to be that way, but sometimes reality does intrude, even on a life that seems to
be something like a fairy tale. With 'N Sync, Joey has
been able to realize almost all of his dreams, which is a
pretty cool thing to have done when you're only twenty-
two. Travel, success, fame, even fortune, and all by doing
something he's always loved to do. He's a perfect ex-
ample of doing something you really love, and then the
money will follow. He's a performer, born and bred.

"I feel most comfortable on stage or in front of the
camera. No matter what I do, I go at it full-tilt and can't
be stopped." But that's the only way to pursue your
dreams.

It's possible that in the future, Joey might also return
to acting. He has the face and the body of a hunk, and
he certainly has the acting experience behind him, not to

mention the talent. So it might not be *too* long before you see him at a theater near you, or switch on your television, and find him speaking, rather than singing. But whatever he undertakes, you know that—just like 'N Sync—he'll give it his all. That's just his way, the only way to be, for the fans and for himself.

JC

Every band needs someone who's serious and focused, the kind of person who tries to keep all the others together. For 'N Sync, that's JC. Not only does he give his all in the stage performances—he's the one with all the acrobatic moves—but in many ways he's the band's lead singer. Not that he'd ever consider himself the *leader* of the band.

"Everyone's got their own role and is a leader in some respect," he emphasized. He's the thoughtful one, the guy who's most often quoted when the group is interviewed. He weighs his thoughts and his words carefully before answering a question.

He knows that at the heart of everything they do is the thought of entertaining their fans, and just like the others, he's more than happy to give the screaming crowds exactly what they want.

"They want to have a good time, and when they go to the show, we just want to entertain the heck out of them." More than that, he realizes that the band has a responsibility to the fans who come to see them. He remembers waiting in line for hours to get tickets to shows (in his case, it was MC Hammer, back when he was big), and the bonding experience of being with other fans. What 'N Sync wants, he said, is "to make sure everybody is safe. As long as nobody is hurtng themselves, there's no harm, no foul."

JC is very much the band's philosopher. He's taken the time to think about the history of music in the Nineties, and why pop has made a real comeback, with the Spice Girls, Hanson, BSB, and 'N Sync. It is, he feels, all to do with trends.

"[Grunge] was just as much of a trend as anything else. They were doing what Mick Jagger and Steven Tyler were doing, which was shaking their heads and running around being wild. They were entertainers; otherwise they would have just sat perfectly still and sang their song. This new generation is great. They want to have fun. And making sure they get that fun is what JC and all the other guys are glad to do. They want pop music to be seen as respectable again.

"It used to be thought of as bubble gum, but it's not anymore," he explained. "The best thing about pop is that it has a little bit of everything in it. Pop can really go in any direction." He wants to make music that affects people, that they'll still be able to love years from now.

"The great thing about music is that everyone hears it in their own way, and every song you hear leaves an impression on you and alters the way you hear everything from that point on."

Joshua Scott Chasez was born to Roy and Karen Chasez in Washington, D.C., on August 8, 1976 (which makes him the second-oldest member of 'N Sync, after Chris). When he was still a baby, his parents moved out of the city, to the suburb of Bowie, Maryland. A couple of years later he was joined by a sister, Heather, and three years after that by a brother, Tyler.

JC enjoyed a very typical suburban upbringing, his time filled with school, family, friends, and church. There was no adversity to overcome, no real hardship of any kind. Everyone treated him well, and in return, JC was good to them, a creed he still lives by: "Treat people the way you want to be treated."

Music was all around the house, even if no one performed. But they did sing together, opening Christmas presents, and Josh, as his parents call him, was exposed to a wide range of music, including classical and jazz.

However, singing wasn't his first love when it came to music; it was dancing. Right from the time he was a toddler, he'd move to the sounds he heard from the radio and the record player. It was an outlet for his natural energy, but even more than that, he was good at it, a natural, and eventually Karen signed her older son up for dance lessons.

If it hadn't been for a dare, JC would probably never have bothered with show business at all. He liked to dance, and loved the lessons, but he was very shy, and not into performing. When he was twelve, he was hanging out at a friend's house when some girls they knew came over. JC and his friend had reputations as good dancers, and the girls wanted the boys to partner them in a talent contest. JC was reluctant, but after his buddy dared him, he couldn't say no. The foursome took first prize, and JC discovered that he enjoyed the performing— and the winning. They entered a couple more contests and won those, and his confidence was rising.

That was when Karen Chasez saw something that would give JC his big break. *The Mickey Mouse Club* was holding open auditions in Washington, D.C. They were actually holding them at venues all over the country, looking for new talent, and would end up seeing twenty thousand kids to fill a total of ten spots.

JC didn't think he had a chance, but went down anyway, along with five hundred others. By the time everyone had been seen, JC was one of the twelve finalists from D.C., which was pretty good going. Then he had to go out to Los Angeles for more auditioning and testing, and was eventually offered a job.

This was amazing news, but if he was going to take it, it would require a lot of changes in the family. Because of work, the Chasez family couldn't just move lock, stock, and barrel to Orlando. The only solution was for Karen to stay in Bowie with Heather and Tyler, and for Roy to move to Orlando with Josh. It was probably just as well that they all enjoyed travel, because suddenly there was a lot of it. The vacation drives they'd taken out West—seeing thirty-eight states in three summer trips— stood them in good stead for all the flying and driving between Florida and Maryland. It was tough for both kids and parents. But it gave JC the opportunity of a lifetime, and he took to it like a duck to water.

"It was one of the best things I could have done," he said of the show. "I got to get my fingers into everything—I wasn't restricted to one thing at all. I got to do comedy, which was fun, and I got to do all kinds of music. If I could do it again, I would."

One thing that Josh wasn't doing, however, was singing. It might seem odd, given that he does so much of it now, but back then he was still very shy when it came to his voice. Karen already knew he had perfect pitch, but JC, although he'd come a long way out of his shell, was still reluctant to sing for people.

"I didn't start singing until I got to Orlando with *The Mickey Mouse Club*," he recalled. "I didn't know that much about music. I just knew that I liked to dance and I started singing cover tunes."

Quite what prompted JC to show his talent is still a mystery. At the prompting of his dance teacher—like any professional, he took lessons to improve his technique— he entered a dance competition, and for some reason decided to enter the vocal competition, too. He didn't have the entrance fee, but his dance instructor paid for him— even though she'd never heard him sing a note.

She kept pestering him to sing for her, but he kept refusing, and until the night of the contest, didn't open his mouth in song for her. The first thing she knew was when he appeared on the stage to sing Richard Marx's hit, "Right Here Waiting for You."

As soon as he began it was quite apparent that not only could JC sing, but that he could sing very well indeed. He needed work to become more professional, but with a vocal coach that was soon happening, and he was singing on *The Mickey Mouse Club*, where one of his friends was Keri Russell (of *Felicity* fame). Within a year, he was also singing on the stage when *Club* performers appeared at Disney World, and in his third year on the television show, he'd gained enough confidence in his own abilities to take solos.

Between performing, rehearsing, school, and traveling back and forth to Maryland during school vacations, Josh had a pretty full schedule. But he realized just how lucky he was to have all of this opportunity, far more than most people. It made him acutely aware of the fact that some had nothing, and he began volunteering some free time at homeless shelters, an idea of service that's stayed with him.

"If you think you had problems," he said, "try living on the streets with your family."

By the end of JC's fourth year with the show, *The Mickey Mouse Club* was winding down, an idea whose time had come and gone. He'd made a lot of friends through it, and one who'd arrived the season before, Justin Timberlake, had become quite a good buddy. Not only did they work and hang together, they also shared the same vocal coach, and a lot of the same attitudes toward music.

JC was a workaholic when it came to learning singing, dancing—anything, in fact. He'd completely throw himself into it, absorbing it, until he'd mastered it. That was the way he also learned how to play guitar and piano—which he still messes around with at home. That workaholism makes him the truly focused one in the band, the one who's always pushing himself to be better and better, to learn more and be able to apply it.

But when *The Mickey Mouse Club* ended, 'N Sync wasn't even a gleam in anyone's eye yet. Josh wanted to do some traveling, to relax, and also to explore the possibilities of a singing career. His first stop was Los Angeles, where a lot of sessions are recorded. He spent a couple of months there, living with friends, getting to know the scene, and even collaborating on the writing of a few songs—something new for him, but which he really enjoyed.

After that he returned to a regular life in Maryland for a while, a chance to decompress and just enjoy life with his family, away from all the pressures of making a television show, a chance to just be a normal person.

From there, JC traveled on to Nashville, to pick up a gig as a singer on song demonstration tapes for a few weeks. Compared to the regular television exposure he'd received, this was very low-key for JC—no one hearing the tapes would even know his name! But anonymity was exactly what he wanted, a chance to develop his voice away from the spotlight. He'd decided that music, and singing in particular, was his great love, the thing he wanted to pursue, and this seemed a good way to start.

That all ended abruptly when he returned to Orlando, and hooked up with Justin, who mentioned that Chris—whom JC already knew—and he were looking to start a band. And from there it was all history.

Success was a lot of work away, but it still came more easily than JC had anticipated. His parents were thrilled for him, of course, particularly because it gave him an opportunity to use his special gifts, singing and dancing, but nobody anticipated that 'N Sync would take off all over the world.

For JC, the biggest problem these days is finding time to sleep. He's someone who enjoys his rest, but when you're due here, there, and everywhere, finding time is difficult.

"You go through the day sleeping fifteen minutes here, twenty minutes there," he explained. "If I sit down for long, my body goes, 'Okay, you're not tired, but you know what? You need to rest just in case.'" And his pillow of choice? Well, during their concerts, fans throw all manner of things onto the stage, and JC says, "I usually keep a stuffed animal from a show to sleep on while we're traveling."

And when he does crash, JC quickly falls into a very deep sleep.

"I fell asleep on the plane and we landed and everything and I didn't know it. Lance had to smack me on the back of the head and go, 'Dude, the plane is empty. You're the last one.' I said, 'Oh, my goodness.'"

That incident, plus a few others like it, along with his serious take on performing and studio perfection, have given JC the reputation of being the old man of the group—which he isn't, of course. But it can still lead Joey to joke, "You see, JC matured too quickly. He peaked at the age of fifteen and he's going downhill slowly. All he wants to do now is sleep!"

Of course, JC isn't going anywhere but up, just like the others. But since they're close friends, they really can rag on each other. And, the truth is, the others are actually grateful that there's one of them who helps keep the others in line.

"He's hardworking and dedicated and a very serious sort of person," is Chris's opinion of his bandmate. "I don't mean he's not any fun, but he knows when it's time to play and when it's time to work. He's really dedicated to his career and that's really admirable."

Singing most of the leads puts JC very much in the spotlight, and like everything else, he takes that seriously. When he's home with his parents, he'll practice his trademark handsprings in the backyard.

But, although he puts on a very adult face, there's still quite a bit of the kid about him, who's happy to get out and throw a football with other guys in the neighborhood.

Another side of him, though, is the loner, the one who'll happily just sit in his room or lose himself in a movie—he remains a mega-fan of the *Star Wars* series, and is eagerly awaiting the new film in the series. But anything with Harrison Ford is also okay with JC—he's watched the *Indiana Jones* movies time after time after time.

His serious attitude has made JC cautious with his money. 'N Sync are a big band, and they've earned a lot in a short time, but he's not one to go out and start blowing what he's made on all sorts of useless things. The one indulgence he allowed himself, after the band made it big, was a Jeep, his dream vehicle. The big problem—the same one all the guys have—is that he doesn't have much time to enjoy it. Success is wonderful, but it does stop any of them from having lives.

So what does JC bring to the mix of influences that make up 'N Sync? His tastes are a little different to the others. He's been exposed to a lot of different kinds of music, and he's drawn from them all. Jazz has given him a love of odd chords and slow songs. From soul and R&B there's Stevie Wonder and Brian McKnight, and from pop he's been influenced by Seal and Sting, whom he calls "brilliant writers." The fact that he can draw on so many sources makes him a very versatile singer, able to work in a lot of different areas, which is something he'd love to do in the future—even if it takes him out of the public eye.

While, like all the others, he has a goal of singing and dancing with Janet Jackson, he can look far enough into the future to see a time when he might not be in front of the crowds. The technical aspects of recording hold a fascination for him—he'll be the one hanging out in the control room, watching the engineer and the producer at work, how they put everything together, and what they do to the voices and the instruments. At some point, he says, he can see himself becoming an engineer. Or, if he chose to invest the money he's earned, he could buy or build his own studio, and take a very active hand in running it.

All that, of course, is a long way off yet. It's the kind of dream that wouldn't become reality until 'N Sync is over, and there seems to be no danger of that happening for a long time. Right now JC is happy to be the voice of sanity in the madness that surrounds the boys everywhere they go. He loves being in the studio, but he also loves performing, getting to display his gymnastic skills on the stage (when he was younger, Josh studied gymnastics, which has helped keep him to limber and lean and moving so smoothly), and relishing the immediate feedback of an audience—even if they're mostly just screaming for the band. It's a rush, there's no doubt about it, and actually meeting the fans, whether before or after a performance, at a CD signing, or on a promotional visit brings it all home to JC just who he's doing it for. Like all of 'N Sync, he knows that the fans have put the band where they are today, and will keep them there in the future. They have a responsibility to their fans, to treat them well, to make time for them, signing autographs and talking.

'N Sync might take up a huge portion of JC's time, but that doesn't mean he has absolutely no life. He does, and it includes a rather odd hobby—stranger, even, that Joey's collection of Superman memorabilia. JC collects menus from the Hard Rock Cafes around the world—he might even be the only person doing so.

In a lot of ways, the menus document his travels with 'N Sync, covering all the corners of the globe, including London, Malaysia, Japan, and Paris. But he also has something very few, if any collectors could boast of owning—a pin of a Hard Rock Cafe menu that he acquired in London. The special pins are distributed to the company to special wait staff who've done exceptional work. JC managed to persuade the woman waiting on him to give her the one she'd been presented with. It took a lot of persuasion, and some consultations with the manager, but eventually he walked away with the treasure, which now has pride of place in his collection.

All that traveling when he was young, and then when he was a regular on *The Mickey Mouse Club* prepared him well for the grueling life of 'N Sync, almost living on airplanes and buses. JC might spend a lot of his time on the road grabbing catnaps when and where he can, but he truly relishes seeing new places. The popularity of the band—and the inevitable mob of girls that gathers around them—makes sightseeing a little difficult, but he's managed to do his share. Something he's learned from his journeys is that while countries and cultures might be very difficult, under the skin we're all very much the same, and all very human, to be treated with respect.

The time on the road has naturally meant that he spends most of his days—and nights—around his bandmates, so it's just as well that they're all the best of friends.

"The best thing about being in the band is the friendship," JC said, "having people around you so you're never lonely."

There's no danger of ever becoming lonely when surround by this group. In fact, you need constant energy to keep up with them (which may be one reason JC takes all those catnaps). They don't really get up to mischief, but they're always ready to be on the go. If they do have some free time away from home, it's usually spent *doing* something, rather than relaxing. For JC, that means inline skating, something all the guys share. Not only is it a great way to keep fit—as JC knows—but it's a wonderful release. And dressed up in a helmet and pads, he has the chance to have a few minutes of privacy away from the fans, which all the boys need once in a while.

In Florida, JC shared a house with Chris, Justin, and Justin's mom, Lynn (he and Chris are roommates in an apartment now). Quite naturally, the place drew a lot of fans from all over. But because JC's parents live well away from all the hullabaloo in Maryland, they managed to avoid the crowds of fans who want to see where the guys live. So when JC does go and see his folks, he really has the opportunity to leave 'N Sync behind for a while. He can go to the store or the mall, drive around, catch a movie, without much of a hassle. It's that time to himself, away from the spotlight, that he values.

JC's family have always supported him in everything he's done, and now he repays them by taking them on the road whenever possible. A few times the whole family has joined him, once or twice both his parents. Usually, however, if someone is going to join him on tour, it's Tyler, who gets to travel during vacations from school. Luckily, Tyler and JC happen to be brothers who get along well; there are none of the usual fraternal arguments. And Tyler gets a remarkable education out of the trips.

One thing JC doesn't have is a girlfriend. There's simply been no time over the last few years to develop a relationship with someone, or even to actually *find* someone special. As you might expect from him, though, JC has a very clear picture of the girl who'd be right for him. Not physically—that's the least important part—but in attitude and personality. He understands that he needs someone who can both complement and counter his natural seriousness, someone who can take him out of himself. The right girl will know, just like JC, when it's time to work, and when it's time to relax. She'll make him laugh—and make sure he has some fun. And, like JC, she'll enjoy going to the theater—but not, he emphasizes, to musicals. According to Chris, however, JC can be really cheesy around girls at times. "He's got all these really bad pickup lines and, I promise that the other day, he actually said to this girl, 'So, do you come here often?' "

Of course, like all boys, he has his fantasy babes.

"I like all sorts of girls but my favorites would be Naomi Campbell because she's absolutely beautiful, and I'm pretty keen on Michelle Pfeiffer—she's gorgeous, I especially liked her as Catwoman."

Oftentimes, however, JC is a guy who'd just rather spend him time around four-legged creatures. His own dog, Grits, died, and when he's on the road, it's not uncommon to find him staring out of the window of the bus at dogs. Sometimes it can be quite funny, according to Chris.

"Say we're driving somewhere and we see a pretty girl on the sidewalk, the four of us will go, 'Hey, check out that girl,' and five minutes later JC will go, 'Wow, check out that dog, what kind is it?' He's nuts about dogs."

Like the rest of the guys in 'N Sync, JC dresses pretty casually, but you'll never find some of the more outrageous clothes favored by Joey in his wardrobe. This is someone who can actually be conservative and dress up in a suit at times, but occasionally funky—sweaters, shirts, team jerseys. "Mostly I just wear whatever's in the closet," he admitted. "I like casual wear because that's what I feel comfortable wearing."

JC, though, is pretty comfortable with every aspect of his life these days, most particularly the band. He knows they're the real deal, a proper band, not just put together to try and sell records. The difference is very important to him, to all of them. They've made it because of their own abilities, their own talent and drive. Not that there hasn't been an element of luck involved; each member of 'N Sync would readily acknowledge that. But even without that, they've had a lot going for them, by the effort they put into everything before even finding a manager. Back then it was JC's gymnastic and dance skills (not to mention Joey's) that led their performances on the stage, until they began working with a professional choreographer.

JC knows full well that he's in a very privileged position, being an international star, a pin-up boy, and he doesn't take it lightly. He wants 'N Sync to be around for many years, bringing pleasure to fans, and gaining new fans as they go. There are literally hundreds of other bands out there, looking for record deals, releasing singles and albums. But JC feels that fans understand that 'N Sync are real, and they've responded to that by making them so popular, that fans can instinctively see the difference between real and fake. Keeping it all real, not getting swept up into all the hype that surrounds the guys, is of paramount importance to him. And to keep doing that, they have to make the music they want to make, the music they would have made whether they were huge or unknown, simply doing it for fun.

If it seems like all the band are down on phoniness, on those who just want to take their fans' money and run, that's because it's true. They were all raised with strong senses of ethics, to respect others—as JC said, "Treat people the way you want to be treated." They were all fans themselves once, and they still are. JC would pay to see Sting or Seal in concert, and a number of others (although the chances are he gets the VIP treatment at any show he attends these days). They understand what it's like; they've seen it from both sides now.

That's one reason JC can stay so focused. Sure, it's a part of his personality, but he also owes it to everyone who's paid to see the band or has bought an album or a single. Each time, they deserve the very best. It's how they can knock themselves out night after night on tour, why JC can survive on just catnaps and still turn in a brilliant performance. He has a reason, and each reason is down there having fun, maybe screaming their names, but above all enjoying the music they're making.

As their fame has grown at home, it's become a little harder for JC to have those quiet times. Though he might miss them, he doesn't mind paying that price; after all, that's one of the reasons they all began this band, why he became an entertainer in the first place. It's in his blood, and he can't deny it—not that he'd try very hard. Whatever happens in the future, it's a certainty that JC will be involved with music and entertaining in some way, whether on record, on the stage—he wouldn't mind doing some acting at some point—or behind the scenes.

LANCE

There's a sixth-grade class in Orlando that has very strong feelings about 'N Sync. They always do their homework, because, every week, those who complete all their assignments compete in a draw for 'N Sync stuff. What makes them so dedicated? And how do they get everything 'N Sync, anyway?

The answer's actually pretty simple—the teacher of the class is Diane Bass, the mother of Lance. She has, you might say, special connections.

Lance Bass might have been the last member to join the band, but he's by no means the least important. If anything, he's exactly what they needed to complete their sound, filling in the bass (no pun intended) end of the vocal harmonies, and offering a very solid bedrock on which the others can build their intricate vocals. Lansten, as the others call him, fitted in from the moment he met Chris, Joey, JC, and Justin, making them into the perfect blend.

Obviously, he didn't just walk in out of the blue and get lucky. He had years of singing experience and training behind him. But he brings more than just his voice to the band. Like JC, he's focused, and he always knows where they're going to be for the next few *months*.

"The guys call me Scoop, because when they ask me about our itinerary I always know!" he said.

Lansten is the organized one. Being on top of things has always been part of his way. And in anything he's done, he's always accomplished it with total, one hundred percent commitment. It's no less with 'N Sync—and it wouldn't work if anyone gave it any less—but now it's paying him the kind of rewards he could never, ever have expected.

Certainly, although Lance loves singing, it's not something he'd ever envisioned as any kind of career. It had long been a part of him, but the idea of show business, of doing this for money, had never really entered his mind.

When James Lance Bass was born on May 4, 1979 in Clinton, Mississippi, his parents, Jim and Diane, already had a three-year-old girl, Stacy. Lance rounded out the family. Clinton was a small town of some 4,000 residents, not far from Jackson, on the west side of the state. There was no big city nearby, no major urban area. Lance grew up like a country boy, used to lots of space around him, the animals and crops of the farms nearby.

His mother, Diane, made her living as a teacher. She'd done a little singing when she was young, and music was always something the family did together, at home, and in the church they all attended, where baby Lance seemed to light up when he heard the children's choir.

It became apparent very quickly, though, that Lance loved to sing and to perform. When he was still tiny, he made his way through "Jesus Love Me," to the astonishment and admiration of his parents, who began to realize that their son had a special gift. Soon he and Stacy were dressing up and putting on shows for their parents, and once he was old enough, Lance graduated to that children's choir at church.

"I grew up singing in church and I always loved singing," he admitted.

But it was far from being the only thing in his life. According to Diane, he was like any kid, who was going to be all manner of things—movie star, restaurateur, company president, and, of course, an astronaut.

The last idea actually stayed with Lance for a long time, even if it did change a little along the way as he grew older.

"I wanted to go into space administration," he confided. "Probably not an astronaut but something in that field."

Singing, however, remained an important part of his life all the way through school, getting slowly more important with each year. Lance's voice matured, and after it broke, deepened a great deal, until he found himself singing the bass parts. In the eighth and ninth grade, he was part of the school show choir. By then it was apparent that his voice shone. He was working with a vocal coach to improve his breathing and his tone, and joined a group called Attache, another show choir.

This was altogether a much bigger deal. The choir toured all over the United States, and took part in competitions against other choirs. So, even before Lance hooked up with 'N Sync, he'd already seen a great deal of the country through the windows of a bus.

Attache was more than just a show choir; they were the top show choir in the country, sweeping competitions, and often on the road entertaining people. While Lance did a lot of signing, more was expected from all the choir members—there were also choreographed routines, which meant that dance lessons became a part of Lance's daily life. After a year with the group, Lance was beginning to think that this was something he could enjoy doing for a living, although going to college was still very much a part of his plan for the future.

So what had prompted Lance to make the move from

singing at home or in church to taking it more seriously? The answer, oddly, was Garth Brooks. Lance saw him in concert when he was fourteen, right as the Stetsoned country singer was really hitting his stride, and was won over by his show. Seeing it, he immediately knew that this was something he wanted to do. His favorite Garth Brooks song is definitely "The Dance." "I like him so much because of the way he performs, and the show he puts on. We'd like to remake 'The Dance' someday," Lance said.

The vocal coach Lance worked with had previously worked with a young man called Justin Timberlake, before Justin went to Orlando to work on *The Mickey Mouse Club*, and Justin had trained with him a little more after the show had ended its run, before 'N Sync got together.

When Chris, Joey, JC, and Justin finally decided they needed a fifth member to do full justice to their harmonies, they looked around for recommendations. One of the people they called was Justin's former voice teacher, who was still working with Lance.

The rest, of course, is history.

Lance had never expected the call. When it came, he was a senior in high school, and making his preparations for college—he'd already been accepted to the University of Nebraska, and he was buckling down, making some very strong grades.

"I always wanted to sing professionally, but I didn't think I would have the chance until they called me up. Right when they called me up was when I was like, 'Okay!'" The fact that it was his voice teacher calling meant that Lance knew this would be cool.

Lance's enthusiasm was one thing, but he still had to deal with his parents. Luckily, they were supportive of the idea of him flying down to Florida to audition with the fledgling band. However, they did insist on one condition: Lance was ready to book his flight and get straight down to Orlando; they insisted he wait a few weeks until school vacation, once Homecoming was over.

Once he finally arrived, there was an immediate bonding between all the guys, even though Lance had never met any of them before. And when they first sang together, without any rehearsal—their first tune was "The Star-Spangled Banner"—it was immediately apparent that they had a very special chemistry, and that Lance fit perfectly into the mix.

It all worked, but one problem remained—what would Lance do? He still had to finish his senior year of high school, and there was a college place waiting for him. There was no way that his teacher/mother would let him abandon all that, and he didn't want to. A compromise was reached, and Lance actually got his high school diploma through independent study, rehearsing with the others in his free time.

In the fall of 1995, before the band really began to take off, he actually did enroll at the University of Nebraska, but only managed to take a few classes before his life started to get hectic, and the boys took off for Europe, on the trip that would see them moving from obscurity to fame and fortune. Not that he's forgotten about college. It's still something he wants to pursue, to get that degree. But he understands that for now it'll have to wait on the back burner, until time permits him to catch up and catch his breath a little.

"I'm in my freshman year of college and it's really hard," he said a few years ago. "I'm taking it one step at a time and I'm trying to get settled with that." He's still a freshman (!), but that will all change in due course.

One talent that Lance never knew he had is for business. Now, with 'N Sync doing so well, he has the chance to investigate that side of things a little more.

"He's really interested in business and marketing and is always on top of things," Joey pointed out. "He could be a business manager some day."

(David Atlas/Retna Limited, USA)

CHRIS

(Bernhard Kuhmstedt)

JC

LANCE

(Larry Busacca/Retna Limited, USA)

Hanging out in NYC

The guys relax before a performance

Putting on another high energy concert

Of course, the band has very good management right now, but in a few years, who knows what could happen—he could even end up working for Garth Brooks on that end of things.

When Lance moved to Orlando, it meant a lot of changes for his family. For Jim and Diane, their baby was leaving the nest sooner than they'd planned, and in a way they'd never imagined. Understandably, they wanted to be close to him, to look after him. His sister, Stacy, was already in college, living away from home. If ever there was a good time to relocate, this was it.

Leaving Clinton for Orlando, however, was a major upheaval. They liked the small-town life, the church and their circle of friends. But blood is always thicker than anything else, and they decided to make the sacrifice to be close to their son, particularly since he wasn't yet eighteen (and still a minor) when he left. So they found a house in Orlando, less than a mile from where all the others were living, and began to settle in. Diane took a year off from teaching, and accompanied 'N Sync on their first trip overseas, one of the chaperones and house moms there to look after them. There was no real need to see that they stayed out of trouble—they were all too well-behaved and over-awed for that. If anything, they were there to make sure nothing bad happened to their charges from the outside. This music business was a new thing to all of them, parents and kids, and the parents were a little wary of it all—probably with just cause, given what had happened to some pop stars in the past.

After a year, however, Diane found herself teaching again, in charge of a sixth-grade class in Florida (now some of the luckiest sixth-graders in America), and now Lance takes to the road unaccompanied by a parent—most of the time. When the chance occurs, usually two or three times a year during school vacations, both of Lance's parents will hit the tour with him for a few days, just to check in, make sure everything's okay, and to see the show—which they genuinely enjoy, in part because it's *their* son up on the stage, entertaining everyone. Obviously, Lance appreciates the support his parents have shown, and their trust, and he repays it handsomely, staying in frequent touch when he's away from home, something that means a great deal to all of them. His sister, Stacy, although she now has her own life, has become one of his biggest fans and boosters.

Lance is probably the most polite, and certainly the shyest of the bunch.

"I'm all right once I know people, but at first I find it really hard." In fact, his usual tactic is to see how people get along with other members of the band first.

"Lance uses us like wild dogs," Joey said. "He holds us by the leash and waits for us to go sniff people out and then he goes and meets them himself." But for someone who is so shy, that's probably not a bad idea, since it means he goes in prepared.

Given his shyness, it might seem odd that Lansten has the reputation as being the most laid-back member of the group, but it's perfectly true. By his own admission, he's "laid-back and friendly" (once he knows you), and he's definitely the least hyper. "JC's always moving around," Justin offered, "but Lance doesn't really do that. He just chills."

In reality, he's very centered. He might still be young, but he knows who he is, where he's going, and what's important to him. Jim and Diane instilled that in both their children when they were still little, and they're proud that neither of them has forgotten or abandoned it. There's a sweetness to Lance that's obvious from his smile. "What you see is what you get" rings true for all the boys, but most especially Lance. He's cleancut (even when he briefly had blue hair), relatively conservative, and comfortable with that. He doesn't need to use his appearance to make any kind of statement. For the most part, he simply wears clothes that feel good, and work with his natural taste. And although he's a good ol' country boy from Mississippi, he quickly points out that he doesn't own either a cowboy hat or boots—well, they just wouldn't be him, would they? He has a very easygoing attitude to every aspect of his look, and there's no vanity about him at all.

"I can't bear looking in the mirror," he admitted. "I guess that's why my hair looks like this!" Mind you, there's never been a bad picture of him yet, so it can't be too terrible. In many ways, he's quite lazy about clothes, the complete opposite of Joey.

"I'm not bothered how I look, except when I'm dating, so I like to look nice when I'm going out," he said.

That opens a whole can of worms—the chance for dating. At the moment that chance just doesn't exist for Lance. What he wants is a real relationship with someone, and with all the pressure and time away from home, that's simply not possible.

"We don't have any girlfriends," he said. "We can see the world, but we can't have girlfriends. That's something we must take." Dating for its own sake doesn't seem to hold much interest for him—going out with any and every girl holds no fascination for him. And when he's on the road, he's there to do one thing—work, not party.

He has an ideal girl in his mind —apart from special babe Jennifer Aniston, whom he admires from afar: "I love her hair, her face, and her innocent looks. I try to watch *Friends* when I can. I practice every Thursday night, which is when it's on, so I only ever see it on tape." But his ideal is a real person, not some girl on a pedestal. Someone who is supportive of what he does (and with him gone a lot, she'd have to be very supportive and understanding), who knows how to have fun and is willing to try new things, like hiking or climbing, or who can just enjoy a day at the beach, Lance's favorite place to relax since he moved to Florida.

"I love the beach," he admitted. "In fact I'm the biggest beach bum and have the legs to prove it—my hairs are bleached blond!"

She would also, like Lance himself, have to be religious. His faith is very important to him, one of the cornerstones of his life, and he'd understandably want to share it with the girl he loves. His own faith came through his parents, who remain quite devout, and Lance hasn't strayed from that path. He doesn't drink (none of 'N Sync drinks), doesn't smoke, and likes to live as cleanly as possible.

That doesn't mean he's a holier-than-thou, goody two-shoes. When he's in the mood, he can flirt with the best of them (and he's constantly around some of the best of them).

"He's pretty good at it and he's sneaky with it too," Chris commented. "You don't really know he's doing it till bam, it's too late." But it's all in fun—Lance never follows through.

Lance is like Joey, in that he's not any kind of major sports fan. He'll shoot some hoops with the guys, even though the admits he's not especially good at the game, and he will try things. Mostly, however, his idea of a good workout is to get on the stage night after night and give each performance his all.

As anyone who's seen them knows, an 'N Sync performance is very high-energy and very physical. The dancing demands a lot of them all, along with the precision of their harmonies. It requires a *lot* of practice, as well as a lot of concentration, and each of the guys needs to be fully psyched up for each and every show if they're going to give the fans what they deserve.

That's where Lance really lights up, "being on stage, performing and seeing all of the people and watching them enjoying and reacting to our music," he said. The joy the band takes in delighting their fans comes through in their smiles, and the fact that a loud audience can push them even higher.

Conquering Europe, and then Asia, was a major thrill for Lance, but he was full of trepidation before the first singles and the album came out in the U.S. "This is our home," he said, "and America is the number one market, it's a major thing to succeed here. But if we don't succeed, we always have the rest of our work, doing our music and everything."

As it turned out, there was absolutely no cause for worry. Success in America couldn't have come more smoothly and quickly, as if the country had just been waiting for 'N Sync to come along—which they had been, in many ways. Having done that, Lance can now look ahead to his next musical ambition, which is for 'N Sync to win a Grammy award—and it could happen—after all, they've won two *Billboard* awards now. There's no denying the impact they've made on the charts and in the concert halls; they've turned into something of an unstoppable force at home.

Everything to do with stardom has been an education for Lance. He was already used to the idea of touring from his time with Attache, and knew that most of it was simply extended stretches of boredom, watching the road or the sky go by and looking forward to the next show. But with Attache he was never in the spotlight the ways he's been with 'N Sync. Now, wherever they go, there's an endless series of interviews, photo shoots, publicity appearances, as well as the concert itself. He's learned how to get by on much less sleep, and also how to present himself to the press.

"We get to do different interviews," he explained. Then, when they read what's published, "We're like, 'Why did we say that?' We look at it and we kind of critique ourselves for the next time. It's a learning experience for us."

One thing all the boys want is to come across as real

people in their interviews. They're all intelligent, articulate, and sensitive guys, with opinions, beliefs, and histories that they want to put across. They're happy to answer the usual questions, the things most fans want to know, but they also want to be able to talk about things in more depth, about the music in particular, which is why they're all doing this in the first place. So, learning how to put that across has been invaluable for them all.

At five feet ten inches and one hundred and fifty-five pounds, Lance would like to be bigger. But it's nothing he gets any kind of complex about. He's a good size and build, and cute as a button with those eyes that are the oddest shade of green. Once you've met him and got to know him, you'll find there's little he doesn't like—with the possible exceptions of phony people, rap (he's not a fan, I'm afraid), and getting up early, which he calls "the worst feeling in the world."

When he finally does have some free time, you can often find Lance in front of the tube, playing video games (one of the common bonds in the band). He's also the most computer-literate of them all, and the only one who spends much time on the Net—although he's certainly not disclosing any screen names he might use—but you should probably check for a Florida ISP.

Like JC, Lance has a soft spot for animals, but he's discovered that the responsibilities of pet ownership and touring don't do too well together.

"I used to have a dog," he said, "but I had to get rid of him because we've been traveling way too much. I couldn't take care of him." However, the story does have a happy ending. Through his mom's teaching, "one of her kids took him, so it was a good thing. He can run around now."

That incident, and the loss of JC's dog, Grits, made the band determined to do something to help strays and abandoned pets. For each tour, 'N Sync will adopt a dog from a shelter, take it on the road with them, and when

the tour is over, prese   y fan—not a bad
souvenir of the grou   ll not only last a
long time, but also   But it's typical of
Lance, who would   ut in the country,
surrounded by ho   although he's not
very good, it's s   do. Back in Mississippi he'd go   year, and always
make sure he went riding—it was his favorite activity.
And no doubt he will—after all, Lansten has been very
good at making dreams come true so far. Not just his
own, but those of a lot of fans of 'N Sync. Which isn't
a bad way to live your life, by any means. But he's
earned his respect, and he values it. The newest member
he might be (although "new" has become relative now),
but he's completely one of the Five Musketeers.

If not for Justin Timberlake's mother, Lynn Harless, there probably wouldn't be an 'N Sync as we know it. She's the woman who's been the den mother to the guys since they first got together—and she's the one who suggested the band name, too, since their voices were so naturally in sync with each other.

It's been very much a family affair for Justin. The band has given him a career. But, it's also helped his mom. For more than a year, Lynn was in many ways their manager, something that gave her a taste for the business, to the extent that she's formed her own management company.

Justin might be the youngest member of the group, but he's definitely not the baby—in fact, he's the one who came into this with possibly the most show business experience, most definitely the widest experience.

Along with JC, he has the soulful lead voice you hear on most of their songs, but he's also a natural harmony singer, able to blend in with or behind the others—a rare talent.

He's also, as many, many people have realized, *the*

cutie of the band. With his big, twinkling blue eyes and blond hair, he's often been singled out as 'N Sync's pinup (to be fair, they're all pretty hot), which can seem a little odd to him sometime, since it's only a couple of years since he had posters of Janet Jackson on his bedroom wall.

At eighteen, he's also the one who's really had to give up a regular life to be a part of the band, leaving school and friends behind to go on the road, and not only undergoing the rigorous schedule of the band, but also finding time to study and complete his high school diploma—no mean feat when you're always exhausted and traveling from one city to another. There's a lot to admire about Justin. He's achieved a great deal, but managed to do it without his head ever swelling, and with his ambition and his soul intact.

He's worked hard for his success—just like the others—but he's been building toward it for years.

Justin Randall Timberlake was born to Randy and Lynn Timberlake on January 31, 1981 in Memphis, Tennessee, making him quite steadfastly a Southerner, and a citizen of one of the most musical cities in the nation, one with a long association to music, back to the blues and beyond. From the very beginning, it seemed as though music was in his blood, which it was, since his father played bluegrass, and little Justin was used to hearing people playing instruments and voices harmonizing all around him.

Just *how* musical he might be was shown when he was only a few months old. His parents would turn on some music, and no matter what the beat, fast or slow, Justin would keep time. That was the first sign. The second, probably even more indicative of the future, came when he was two and a half years old. The family was driving home from a bluegrass festival, with the radio playing in the car. Suddenly Justin began signing along with the radio—not the main vocal line, but adding a harmony! It was unusual, but it meant that he could hear things in music that many people couldn't.

Not long after that, Justin's parents divorced, and he lived with his mom, Lynn, who would eventually marry Paul Harless, although Justin does keep in regular contact with his dad, Randy, and his new wife, Lisa.

While that was a change that hurt for a long time, there was one constant in his life—church. Going back at least two generations, Justin's family had been strong church singers, and as soon as he was old enough, he joined them. It was apparent, though, that his voice was far better than most of the congregation.

"I grew up singing in church," he said. "Then I got into voice lessons when I was about eight. Then I did talent shows and things, and from that moment on, I knew that's what I wanted to do." It wasn't just a case of "doing" talent shows—Justin was winning them with his singing and his natural dancing. They took him all over Tennessee, including one memorable performance at the Grand Ol' Opry—the stage so many have aspired to perform on.

Still, Justin's first *real* taste of what it would be like to be a star came in the fourth grade, when he and some friends put together a band to lip-sync to songs by New Kids on the Block, who were then the hottest thing in music (another taste of the future: they worked with Johnny Wright, who'd become 'N Sync's manager). They took part in a show at their school, all dressed for the part, and then they were asked to perform at a neighboring school. Family connections provided a limo for them to arrive in style. They did their show, and found themselves pursued by screaming girls. It was only the quick action of a teacher, hustling them into an empty classroom, that kept them safe!

Apart from music, Justin's obsession when he was younger—and still today—was basketball. His idol at the time was Michael Jordan, which led him to become a fan of the North Carolina Tarheels—Jordan's alma mater. "I collect North Carolina Tarheels basketball gear," Justin has admitted. "I love basketball and whenever I have the chance, I play like crazy." While he's good—all that practice has paid off—at six feet even, he's too short to ever be more than a pickup player.

His experiences in the talent shows and his short-lived group prepared him for what was the logical next step— trying to get on *Star Search*. The television show was something of a national, televised talent contest, a place where Justin could show his gifts to the whole country.

It all began with a talent search for the show in Justin's hometown of Memphis. Naturally, he went along, and found himself chosen to participate on the show. That was when the coincidences really began to happen . . .

Star Search was filmed in Orlando. On the next sound-stage, Justin and Lynn discovered, *The Mickey Mouse Club* was taped. Justin was a big fan of the show, and had been for a while. The idea of performing on it had been something of a dream for him. While touring the set, he was told that they would be holding open auditions across the country for new performers—and one of the cities where they'd hold the auditions would be Nashville—across the state of Tennessee, a few hundred miles from Memphis.

Justin didn't win *Star Search*, but it did give him a huge amount of exposure, and confidence for what would be his biggest test so far—impressing the casting director for *The Mickey Mouse Club*.

That year, thirty thousand kids across America auditioned to fill seven places on the show. In Nashville, Justin Timberlake was one of them, one who found himself suddenly one of the new cast members.

His acceptance would mean big changes for Justin, as well as Lynn and Justin's stepdad, Paul. There was no way Justin could commute from Memphis to Orlando every week, which left the family only one option—a move farther south, and that was exactly what they did, with Lynn pregnant with Jonathan, who'd come along in 1993 (there's also another, younger brother, baby Steven).

"In the Disney Studios I also found new friends, and I could prove my talent as a singer and dancer," Justin explained. One of the friends he made was Josh Chasez, JC to his buds. He was four years older than Justin, but the two of them just seemed to hit it off perfectly, as if there was no age difference at all.

Justin came into the show in 1992, but JC was already a veteran, and ready to show his new friend all the ropes.

"JC was on the show for four years," Justin said, "and I joined two years after that. So, actually, together, we did the show for two years, over on Sound Stage One."

Florida was a big learning curve for Justin, in every sort of way. That included his introduction to romance, when he was in the sixth grade. Well, maybe it wasn't heavy duty romance, but certainly his first kiss. It was with a girl called Mindy, who also worked at Disney. They were at a party, when she kissed him, and "I had butterflies in my stomach." One kiss was the limit, though, and nothing ever developed between Justin and Mindy.

Between the show, tutoring on the set, playing basketball, and voice and dance lessons, Justin had a pretty full schedule in Florida. But he was taking everything in, becoming a better performer every week.

The only problem was that after he'd been with the show for two seasons, *The Mickey Mouse Club* was taken off the air, and in 1995, at the age of fourteen, Justin found himself unemployed! Of course, thanks to his connections with JC, Joey, and Chris, that didn't last for long.

Justin believed in the new group, and so did Lynn. Even though she had a baby to look after, she threw

herself into helping them. Long before they hooked with
with Johnny Wright and Lou Pearlman, it was Lynn who
was looking after their affairs, helping them organize
their rehearsals, some early performances, and their demo
CD and video. Without her help, they'd have been lost.
Even for her, this was something completely new—she'd
never managed a band before! What she did went above
and beyond the call of duty. Not only was she looking
after the band, she was also housing three of them. Apart
from Justin, both JC and Chris lived in the Harless house
until the spring of 1998, when they got their own places
in Orlando.

It was probably natural that Lynn would be so involved. Justin was still only fourteen, and she wasn't
about to let him take to the road without being there to
look after him. In fact, for the first year and a half, she
was constantly on the road with 'N Sync. She'd suggested the name, handled their affairs, been their chap-
erone and advisor—to all intents and purposes, she was
the sixth member of the band, every bit as important as
the guys on the stage.

When she finally handed over her managerial responsibilities for 'N Sync, she discovered that she'd developed a taste for the business, and opened her own
management company, which she runs while looking after Steven and Jonathan, taking on the girl group Inno-
sense as her first clients—they now also have a deal with
RCA, 'N Sync's American record company, and they do
their recording at Lou Pearlman's Trans Continental studio in Miami.

Justin didn't mind his mother being with them all the
time. He said, "it just means that my mom's always
there, like she would have been, had I been
home. . . . She's still my mom, and she'll tell me what to
do, but she's cool."

It was during the early days of the group that Justin
feel in love for the very first time, with a girl called

Danielle. He met her through friends from *The Mickey Mouse Club*, and they were together for nine months, until a friend told him that she was also dating someone else.

"She ended it," he recalled sadly, "even though I never hurt her. Danielle broke my heart . . . I still can't forget what Danielle did to me." It was enough to put him off romance for a long time—he's still in no hurry to find someone new.

Of course, these days Justin simply has no time for romance anymore. He's always on the road or in the studio. And on those couple of days a month that he has off, well, he's happy to spend those with his family.

The idea of family is very important to Justin. Both he and his mom carry cell phones, so they can always be in touch with each other. He might be grown, he might be very famous, but to her he's still her son, her boy. While it's impossible for him not to feel pressure, given his schedule, she wants to keep that pressure as light as possible, reminding him that he can walk away any time he wants.

There have been times he wished he was back at school, free of the responsibilities he now has, but those times soon pass.

"We all get homesick, but we don't really talk about it," he said. "Anyway, the five of us are like a family and we all look out for each other." When he's not homesick, Justin realizes this group is the very best thing that could have happened to him, giving him the chance "to make music, meet people and travel."

The way things have gone, with 'N Sync's ascent to stardom, has surprised him. "It's growing rapidly and we're very pleased with the progress we've made," he said. "We're nothing but happy and we love our fans."

All of them are learning as they go along, always interested in making what they do better for the fans, and for themselves, too.

"When we see ourselves on TV, we start critiquing from the minute we see it, and we want to keep taking steps forward." The special moments come at shows when fans start singing their songs back to the band. "To know that you've touched them enough that they listen to your songs so often that they know them by heart—that's special."

While it's generally a blast, being in 'N Sync can also occasionally be hazardous to your health, as Jason has discovered. Rehearsing for a European tour, he was practicing a somersault, landed badly, and broke his wrist. This was something very serious, given how acrobatic and precise the band's routines are.

"It was a nasty misfortune," he said. "I heard a crack in the hand and it hurt me so much." He was rushed to the emergency room, where his wrist was X-rayed, then put in a cast. The incident raised some terrible questions: Would Justin be able to perform? What would happen to all the routines they'd worked out?

In the end, he was able to perform, by being careful.

"Sure, it hurts sometimes, but I get painkillers and the main thing is that the tour was good," Justin said when it was all over. It was enough to make them think carefully, to try and avoid any more broken bones.

For all that, Justin remains very athletic. Give him a spare hour and if he's not sleeping, the chances are he'll be shooting some hoops.

"I love basketball and whenever I have the chance, I play like crazy," he admitted. And, usually when he's playing, he'll wear the blue and white of UNC—his favorite colors. Even if he doesn't chance to play some round ball, he'll find some kind of exercise, because "working out always puts me in a calmer state of mind," he explained. It's a chance to focus some of that energy that builds up over the hours of sitting in buses and planes with no real outlet. While the most important thing is performing, exercise is a real release for all the boys.

Justin's other big release is going to stores. "I'm also a shopaholic," he said quite readily. Apart from his collection of North Carolina basketball stuff, he loves to shop at a store called Just For Men, "which sells suit jackets and real smart stuff, I like to shop there." Lance isn't the only one who can dress conservatively and smartly! Of course, most of the time, Justin is very casual in his approach, in athletic gear, baggy jeans—pretty much the same as the rest of the guys, although definitely *never* as weird as Joey's outfits. If there's one particular item of clothing he likes, though, it would be sneakers— he currently has about twenty different pairs.

Still too young to really think about buying his own place, when Justin turned seventeen, he did allow himself one big indulgence—a new car. Well, not exactly a *car*; he treated himself to a Mercedes van, painted a sweet candy apple red and "all chromed out"—he's even added shiny rims to it now. When he's home, he can often be found it in, cranking the tunes—one thing he made sure of was that it had a bangin' stereo system— and enjoying some quiet time off by himself, anonymous in traffic. So if you're in Orlando and see a red Mercedes van, there's a pretty good chance it'll be Justin on the freeway.

That's his luxury, his present to himself for all the work he's put in and the success that's happened. Who can blame him for allowing himself a treat? Of course, he's also given things to family and to the close friends he's had for a long time.

Inevitably, as in any successful band, he's been forced to become suspicious of strangers who want to get friendly. The people who knew him before this are one thing; he can trust them. The new "friends," though, all too often only want to know him because of what he is, not who he is. And though Justin is incredibly mature for his age, he is still quite young. So all the members of 'N Sync watch out for each other and keep their distance from "fake people." As they've said, they're like their own little family, all brothers together. The Five Musketeers—all for one, and one for all!

When Justin finally finds the girl of his dreams—and not one who'll end up cheating on him—he's developed clear ideas of what she'll be like. Self-confidence is of paramount importance. He doesn't need someone who's timid and insecure. But at the same time, she should know the fine line between confidence and overconfidence, and not cross it. One is appealing, the other a real turn-off for Justin. To deal with him, or any of 'N Sync for that matter, she'd better have a good sense of humor, and of fun. She'd also better be spontaneous, and able to cope with someone who, on the spur of the moment, might suggest going bungee-jumping (which he has done) or rock climbing. And it goes without saying that she'd better be a basketball fan—the winter months would be *very* long otherwise.

Kids, too, had better be a part of her plan, as Justin is quite devoted to his younger brothers. When he's off the road, he spends a lot of time with them. By the very nature of his stature and his age, they really look up to him. Five-year-old Jonathan has already seen the band several times, and even imitates his big brother, putting on shows for his parents at home. So when Justin finally does settle down, it's a certainty he'll be wanting a brood of his own.

It says a lot about how romantic he is that "my favorite actress is Sandra Bullock but I like Tyra Banks too because she's beautiful."

It's not just in the movies that romance attracts him. His biggest musical influence is Brian McKnight, who's put out more than one or two romantic ballads of his own. If you listen carefully, you can certainly here that edge in Justin's own voice, and the emotion he brings to his favorite 'N Sync song, "God Must Have Spent a Little More Time on You." Actually, at some point he'd love to work with McKnight, or even other idols like Jermaine Dupri—an overall band favorite—and the legendary Stevie Wonder.

Which isn't to say that other singers don't blow him away. Like Janet Jackson, with whom the band toured last year.

"[Manager] Johnny Wright just came in and said, 'C'mon man, you're gonna open for Janet Jackson,' and I went 'Oh, my God!'" It was one of the highlights of his life, and for one simple reason—crushing. "I'm in love with Janet Jackson," he admitted at the time. "Probably about two or three years ago I had her poster on my wall, so I'm pretty infatuated."

Meeting her and working with her was a dream come true every day—and if they ever should record together, that'd be his idea of heaven.

For now, though, he has plenty to concentrate on, entertaining his own fans every night. From being a fan, Justin has moved to being a poster on the walls of lots of people, and also an inspiration to them. He might still be young, but he takes all that very seriously. There are people paying money to buy his records, to watch him perform, and that means he owes them.

His biggest thrill still comes from being in front of an audience, in entertaining them, and most specifically when they sing the words back to the band. That's a feeling like no other, knowing this audience is there for *him*, that he's doing something very right.

In part because of his mother's involvement with the band, and also because of the other guys, there's no way all this is going to Justin's head. His faith, which is important to him, would never allow it anyway. He might be idolized, but he's definitely not an idol (he's not idle, either, come to mention it!). He has plenty of very human qualities, not the least is annoying all the others with his ability to burp at will, and the constant clearing of his throat which seems to happen during interviews. And, for whatever reason, Justin has a huge fear of reptiles. Lizards, chameleons, you name it. But the thing that really terrifies him is snakes. "No reptiles! None whatsoever. I will not ride the tour bus!" he announced when the others joked that they'd be bringing a snake on the road with them.

He also has one very endearing habit, although it does stop him ever being able to keep secrets.

"I talk in my sleep a lot. My mom used to laugh at me because if she wanted to find out something about me, she'd come in while I was sleeping and start talking to me." He still does it, although the chances of finding anything out are more remote these days, given that the guys only average about four hours' sleep a night when they touring.

Like JC, Justin loves dogs, and has two of his own at home, Scooter and Ozzie, as well as two cats, Millie and Alley—so he's completely in favor of the band's plan to rescue animals from shelters, their own small contribution to the welfare of pets.

Really, it's not only Justin who's become successful, but his whole family. Through his achievements, they're all enjoying something. Yes, they have the fans knocking at their door, but they treat them with respect, because they understand how much Justin means to the people who've traveled a long way—often from other continents—to get a glimpse of his home. And the fact that he's been able to do all this while still maintaining his integrity has been important to Lynn and Paul. They don't want to lose their son, the boy who's always been so good and kind—just a genuinely nice person—to all the fame. Whenever he comes home exhausted, he's still the same person who left. As much as he loves the life he lives (and really, while he might fantasize about going back to high school and playing B-ball, there's no way he'd really do it), he's never going to change. The basic values run too deep within him. He can separate the stage from reality.

That's the beauty of the band, however; they're *all* that way, remarkably mature in the attitude they bring to the way they work. Yes, they have fun, but all of them, not just JC and Lance, know when it's time to get serious. And they give it everything they've got, every time, for the fans.

Although he's the youngest, Justin has probably changed least of all the guys, certainly on the outside. Where Chris has grown out his hair and colored it, and Joey's grown his goatee, and JC and Lance have definitely changed their hairstyles (JC's gone very smooth, while Lance has turned spiky), Justin remains pretty much the same as he was almost three years ago—a little blonder, perhaps, but nothing extravagant.

Justin's closest friends have become the other members of the band. At first that might not seem like much of a surprise. After all, he spends most of his time with them, and has for the last three years. He knows them almost as well as his own family, and they know him just as well. But that same fact could easily mean that once he has the chance to get away from them, he'd jump at it. Spending *so* much time in small spaces with four others could make him, yearn to be alone.

But when Justin does get his privacy, which, in all fairness, he relishes (although, with 'N Sync now so big at home, he can't just vanish to the movies anymore without a mob scene), he finds himself on the phone with. . . . who else? Either Joey, Lance, JC, or Chris. He and JC do share a special bond that goes back to *The Mickey Mouse Club*, but that's been extended to everyone else.

Nor have Justin and JC forgotten their old friends from Disney. Some, like Keri Russell, have gone on to their own success (she's television's *Felicity*, as if you could ignore the fact). Some have been seeking success, and have found a helping hand from 'N Sync. Like Brittany

Spears, who's a phenomenal singer—and who just happened to be one of the opening acts on the first leg of 'N Sync's debut American headlining tour at the end of 1998, along with girl group Wild Orchid. These are guys who remember, and who are eager to help other people along—and you certainly can't fault that.

So what's in the future for Justin? A few years ago, back when he was still a Mouseketeer, he saw a performing arts degree in his future. It was, he thought, something that would offer long-term help to his career. Now, of course, that career has had the kind of boost that happens to very few people. He can't get much higher. Down the line a few years, however, college remains a strong possibility for Justin, to offer him new experiences. And in return, of course, he'll even be able to teach the class a few things. For right now, though, the band is most definitely the thing. . . .

THE BAND

When Chris first hooked up with Joey, and they sang together, they immediately knew they had something very special going on. Their voices blended *so* well, it was as if they'd always been doing it. Putting a group together around them was Chris's idea, and he was the one who found JC and Justin.

JC and Joey already knew each other.

"Being down in Orlando, you're bound to run into people," JC explained. "Joey and I met each other because he used to go to high school with Jennifer McGill who was on *The Mickey Mouse Club*. That's how we met. . . ."

In fact, as JC explained, in the wake of 'N Sync and the Backstreet Boys, Orlando has become something of a pop Mecca.

"Now that everything's been happening everyone's trying to get a gig," he said. "There's [always] been a lot of talent down there because of the theme parks. A lot of people go down there to the stage shows, and there's a recording studio which brings a lot of musicians down there. Plus, Miami is a four-hour drive away. It's pretty packed with talent. It's just undiscoverable because everyone is working at the theme parks.''

The four of them pretty quickly proved to have a magical, indefinable chemistry together, particularly with Justin's natural, soulful ability to sing harmony on the songs. From the very first, his mother, Lynn, was behind them all the way, taking over their management, and helping to organize the rehearsals for the quartet, and even giving them their name, 'N Sync, because their voices were so in sync with each other.

Lynn was great, but she had no experience in the business, as she well knew. The first goal was to get an act together, some songs and some dancing, then find a manager who would really be able to push them. So, beginning in the summer of 1995, as soon as they got together, the boys put themselves through some punishing routines to work out and perfect everything.

"Every day it was a four-hour routine," JC explained. "Joey would get off work at around nine o'clock at night, and we'd go into this warehouse and we'd rehearse from like, nine to twelve, or nine to one—straight dancing and singing all night." That requires a great deal of dedication, and it was obvious from the very beginning that they were all fully committed to this. Four hours a day would have been a lot, but they were also slotting in vocal rehearsals whenever they had time, and meanwhile Joey and Chris were also doing their own full-time gigs at Universal. No one was taking this lightly. They were fully focused, they had their goals, and they knew the standard they needed to achieve to make it all happen. As Justin said, "We all had to make sacrifices, but to us they were small sacrifices compared to what we've gotten to do."

They were improving every day, but there was still something missing. What they needed, they figured out, was someone with a low range, who could fill out the bass end. The only problem was that they didn't know anyone with a voice like that. So where would they find somebody?

They began making calls, to everyone they could think of. There were plenty of good voices, but finding someone with a good bass voice was proving to be very difficult. Finally, "We called Justin's vocal teacher, and he recommended Lance," Chris recalled.

Lance was eager, but at the same time understandably a little hesitant. Here was a chance, but it was in Florida, not his home of Mississippi. But vacation time was coming, and as soon as he was done with school, he headed down. From the moment they all met, it seemed that the chemistry was just as strong with Lance as it had been before.

The first song the new quintet sang was "The Star-Spangled Banner," and Lance's voice fit in as if it had been made to be a part of this group—which it probably had.

He was in. Or, rather, he was in once his parents approved of the idea. He immediately began rehearsing with the others, working twice as hard because he had a lot of catching up to do. The five were pushing themselves to the limit. They knew they had unlimited potential, and they were eager to take advantage of it.

On Lynn's advice, they were going into the studio to record a demo CD and a video—these days no one would take demo cassettes seriously anymore. And why the video? Well, they wanted the demo to show the full range of their talents, that they could sing outside a recording studio, that they could dance, and also—since, let's face it, it *is* important—that they were cute; cute does help boy bands. The CD had them singing some songs they'd written and arranged themselves, to show their abilities in that area, as well as one cover, of the Beatles' "We Can Work it Out."

It took several months of rehearsal, until the end of 1995, before they were ready to go and make the demos.

Since it was their own money they were investing in this project, they wanted to be well-prepared. Even then, it was all being done on a very tight budget—no one had money to spare. So it was all stripped to the bone, no special effects, just five voices, five faces, five dancers. What they wanted to do, in effect, was sell themselves, and the best way to do that was to show exactly what they could do, not hide behind instruments and intricate effects.

Finally, it was complete. They had something to show people. Their initial plan, with Lynn's full approval, was to find a manager who knew the business well, who could help them get a recording contract, which was what they'd need if a lot of people were going to hear them. Some research brought the names of plenty of potential managers, and 'N Sync mailed out their demo packages. Then they waited and hoped.

Early in 1996, a copy of the demo reached Lou Pearlman, who also lived in Orlando. When he was young, Pearlman—the cousin of Art Garfunkel, of Simon and Garfunkel fame—had been involved in music. He'd played guitar and had a band, which got as far as opening for people like Kool and the Gang and Donna Summer. Then he'd abandoned it all for the serious business of college, where he earned an MBA (at Queens College, with Jerry Seinfeld as a classmate), and then went on to study law.

From there he became something of an entrepreneur, getting into the aviation business, leasing jets to any number of acts—Michael Jackson, Paul McCartney, and New Kids on the Block. Airplanes to airships was a small step, and soon Pearlman owned a number of advertising blimps.

It was the New Kids, though, who got him thinking seriously about music again, at the encouragement of his cousin. When Pearlman learned the kind of business a band like New Kids on the Block was doing, he became very interested. Not with the idea of performing himself, but with being a manager.

Pearlman was the one who discovered the Backstreet Boys, and who invested a lot of his money in them in the early days—he claims that his initial investment in the band was three *million* dollars. However, while he was eager and keen, he didn't have the background in the music business to put real success together. A first BSB single saw some minor action in America, but the musical tastes of the country were still mired in grunge. America wasn't really ready for pop music yet.

Pearlman needed some help, and it came in the form of Johnny and Donna Wright. Johnny had known singer Maurice Starr back in the Eighties, when Wright was a radio disc jockey in Boston. The two had kept in touch, and when Starr offered him a job working with New Kids on the Block—essentially being their road manager— he'd accepted. Along the way, he learned a great deal from their manager, Dick Scott. When the New Kids fell apart, Johnny and Donna moved south, to Orlando.

It was probably fate that Johnny, Donna, and Lou should meet. At first Johnny was reluctant. He'd been involved with one big teen group. But with Donna's encouragement, the three of them got together to work on the future of BSB.

Johnny Wright was familiar enough with the business to realize that trying to crack America was a waste of time. "I decided, let's send them over to Europe and see if we can build a story for them over there." It would work, he believed, because Europe was more open to pop. Take That were massive, East 17, and the Spice Girls were quickly becoming mega. More than that, the Backstreet Boys would go in with an advantage, because "a lot of these groups like that weren't singing, and we were taking a group that could really sing."

As everyone knows, it paid off in a huge way.

'N Sync weren't aware of that, however, when they

sent their demo to Lou Pearlman. Given the fact that Orlando isn't *that* big, they'd probably heard of the Backstreet Boys, but had no idea what was happening with them, or that Lou was even involved with that band.

By that time, BSB were in Europe with Johnny Wright, really starting to make a major splash.

Lou was immediately impressed by this new group. They looked good, they could dance, and they could obviously sing very, very well. He had them come into his office so they could sit and talk, and he liked the way they presented themselves, not as five individuals, but as a band. By then of course, they'd been working together for several months, and they really were a unit.

After some thought, Lou phoned Johnny Wright in Germany to tell him about his new discovery. Initially it seemed too good to be true, that Orlando could be home to two excellent boy bands, but that was the truth. Johnny knew Lou well enough to realize he wouldn't exaggerate, and he flew back across the Atlantic to check out this new find.

After seeing them and hearing them, he had to agree with his partner. There was talent to spare in the five-piece, and plenty of possibility for the future. They'd brought themselves a long way, although there was still a lot of polishing to be done. They sat down with 'N Sync, Lynn, and Lance's parents—he was still under eighteen at the time—and said they'd be willing to manage the band. There were no guarantees, of course—in the music business, how could there be?—but they'd do their best, and they had a track record to show they knew what they were doing with this kind of music.

For the band, it was like a dream come true. They couldn't have found anyone better to handle their careers. Lynn happily stood aside; these people had contacts it would have taken her years to make, and she believed they'd do their best for the boys.

The potential was there, but Lou and Johnny wanted

to hone it before they approached any record companies. So they had the boys recording demos at Pearlman's studio in Orlando, learning how to work properly in the studio. And when they weren't doing that, they were learning about dancing from one of the very best in the business, Robert Jaquez, who'd worked with Janet Jackson, Prince, and Michael Jackson—three people who really knew how to move!

"We worked all the beginning of '96, just rehearsing every day," JC recalled, "and then, in the summer of '96, that's when we got our deal."

Of course, it wasn't *quite* as easy as that. 'N Sync were talented, and the constant rehearsals had given them a real shine, but record deals didn't just fall from the sky. They still had to play some shows. To be fair, they were all seasoned performers, used to entertaining people, but they'd never done it together, as 'N Sync. A few small shows around Florida helped them get used to being onstage together, to putting into action all the moves they'd spent so long practicing. The shows did something else, too—they gave the band confidence in their abilities. They could see that it hadn't all been time spent in vain. People responded to them, applauded and cheered them, and that was precisely the boost they needed.

With the Backstreet Boys taking off so strongly in Europe, Johnny Wright was a person who could get the ear of people at record companies there. He and Lou Pearlman had already decided that Europe would be a good place for 'N Sync. America still wasn't getting into boy bands. The new pop music hadn't taken hold yet. And it wasn't as if 'N Sync were BSB clones. They had their own identity as a band, in their voices and their extremely acrobatic moves. 'N Sync would do well in Europe; the continent was primed and ready for an act like them.

One label that was extremely interested was BMG in Germany, one of the biggest record companies in the world. They'd been the European home to Jive, BSB's label, until Jive split. And that meant they were looking for a top boy band, someone they could work with. Lo and behold, along came 'N Sync.

Still, their demo and their act had to satisfy the label's suits, the people who made the decisions. They sent on the material, and spent time waiting, biting their nails (at least, the boys with that as their bad habit), and hoping. This was big, this was important. If the deal came through, they were really on their way. And if it didn't . . . well, they didn't want to think about that.

Finally, after what seemed like forever, BMG called Lou Pearlman, who was now installed as 'N Sync's business manager. 'N Sync had a record deal. He called the boys, and suddenly, it was time to party.

It wasn't a party that could last too long, though. "Two days after we signed the contracts, they said, 'Pack your stuff, we're leaving,' " Justin recalled. And that's exactly what they were doing; it was time to break out the passports and prepare for something new; 'N Sync were on their way to Europe. The dreams just kept coming true, one after another, after another. How much better could it get, they all wondered. And the answer seemed to be, wait and see.

Europe was new to them all. A different language, different customs, a sense of being foreigners met them for the first time as they settled in Germany, the home of BMG.

"We went to Munich, Germany, for a year and a half," said Joey. That was where they were based. In that year and a half, they'd do a lot of traveling. But the first plan of action was to have the band working with some songwriters and arrangers, preparing material for their first album. They didn't actually do any of the recording in Germany, but it served as a central jumping-off point, close to everything else in Europe.

One of the producers tapped for the project was Denniz Pop, who had his own studio, Cheiron, in Stockholm, Sweden. He did a lot of work with writer Max Martin; the two of them together had become quite a team. Most recently they'd worked with the Backstreet Boys and Robyn, two of the hottest teen acts, and going back a few years, they'd been responsible for the hits from Ace of Bass—not a bad track record at all.

The first tunes 'N Sync would be recording would be up in Sweden, with Pop at the controls. The vocal arrangements had already been carefully worked out by the time the band arrived in Stockholm. All the boys would need to do was sing over the instrumental track for the song that had been earmarked as the first single, something to test the waters before recording the complete album.

It went better than anyone could have anticipated.

"BMG reserved a whole week for us here to record our first single, 'I Want You Back,'" Justin recalled. "But it only took seven hours. The rest of the time we had fun in Stockholm."

In this day and age of perfection, laying down a full set of perfect vocal tracks in just seven hours is little short of miraculous. The record company's budget of a week was actually quite reasonable. But it showed just how good 'N Sync had become, and how professional they were. They were happy with the results they heard over the studio monitors.

"We thought it was something cool, because we think our voices have more of an R&B feel," recollected JC. "But when you mix it with that dance beat you put under it, it's something really different, and you get so many cool things, like the harmonies and the little riffs and things. It's like a mix between a break beat and a hip-hop feel, and it's something you can really dance to."

While they were in Sweden, the band also recorded another song, also co-written by Max Martin, called "Tearin' Up My Heart," which was also full of commercial potential. All in all, their two weeks in Sweden (BMG had given them a week per song) had been very fruitful.

Of course, that wasn't the only recording they'd be doing. Songs had been solicited from a number of writers, and different producers had been enlisted to give a varied feel to the 'N Sync sound. With their R&B feel, it made perfect sense to everybody that the band should work with a lot of American producers, and so, in the late spring of 1996, the band found themselves shuttling back to Florida to work on plenty more tracks. For the album, and to fill out the singles.

They had a limited amount of time for recording, so it was perhaps just as well that much of it was done at their home base in Orlando, either at Lou Pearlman's Trans Continental, where they already felt comfortable, or at Parc or House of Hits studios, which, again, were close to where they lived. In there they found enough time to fly up to New York to do a couple of tracks with the Full Force crew—too good an opportunity to turn down.

"We were all excited for it to be happening so fast, but we weren't exactly ready," remembered Chris. "We had to put the album together in about two or three months, sometimes recording a song a day."

And when they weren't busy in the studio, they found themselves on the phone, doing interviews with German magazines, as the record company began a push prior to the first single coming out there.

"I Want You Back" was the unanimous choice, and it made perfect sense. It was catchy, upbeat, a dance tune that was also a pop song. It kicked, and played well both on the radio and in the clubs.

"The song is about suddenly finding yourself separated from the person you feel so deeply about because you've done something stupid to screw it up. I think it hits people because they can relate to it like a love song, but it's powerful and up-tempo enough to kick them, too," JC said.

There was the aching of the verses, with some killer harmonies, where the real R&B feel came from, over a relentless hip-hop beat, that really kicked after the choruses. The slow bridge just accented the helpless feeling of the song, before coming back in with the beat and the high harmonies that were low in the mix.

All in all it was a perfect little slab of pop music, as contagious as the measles, as infectious as a cold, but a lot nicer to get. It was released in Germany in September, 1996, and in its first week alone, scored an incredible *six hundred* airplays on the radio, shooting straight into the Top 100 singles chart. In fact, it broke all kinds of European records, becoming the fastest-rising single *ever*, better than anything Michael Jackson (the previous holder of the title) had ever achieved, and becoming the longest-lasting single ever on the charts by a new band even though it never hit the top spot. It simply wouldn't go away.

Certainly the performance of the disc impressed BMG. Their president, Thomas Stein, said, "I have hardly ever witnessed newcomers enter the German charts with such incredible, rocket-like speed," which was high praise indeed, given the fact that BMG was one of the big six record companies in the world, and Stein had seen plenty of bands come and go in his time.

Of course, he was a little biased, since 'N Sync was signed to Ariola, a BMG label, but the fact that the single sold more than 350,000 copies spoke for itself. Right from the word go, 'N Sync was established as a heavy hitter on the scene.

As it eventually began to fade, it was followed up by the other song recorded in Sweden, "Tearin' Up My Heart," produced this time, not by Denniz Pop, but by his protege, Kristian Lundin, which he'd co-written with Max Martin. Once more it proved that the Swedes understood pop music, which had been evident since the heyday of Abba in the Seventies, through Ace of Base, to Robyn, Aqua, and the Cardigans. The song wasn't quite as uptempo as "I Want You Back," propelled by a funky bassline that popped, and a xylophone under the full chorus that acted as a real hook. It gave more expression to the harmonies of the boys. But it was the chorus that was the charm, exploding out of the chorus, completely dressed and ready for the dance floor. There simply wasn't a thing wrong with it. The arrangement had something all good pop music should have, the tension of the verses building to the release of the chorus, a bridge that took the song in another direction, and the whole thing resolved itself on some lovely synthesizer chords to finish it off, rather than fading away on repetitions of the chorus. If the first single showed that 'N Sync was a force to be reckoned with, this fully established their reputations. Like its predecessor, it sold more than 350,000 copies—truly a staggering amount for Germany—and rose to number ten on the charts. Still not the top spot, but that would simply have been the icing on the cake.

Nor was it just in Germany that the band was doing well. The singles were breaking out all over Europe, making waves on the charts in Sweden, Switzerland, Austria, Holland, and Hungary. Two records into their career, 'N Sync could justifiably claim they were an international sensation.

One thing they were not going to be, however, was a studio band. On the heels of the single, they announced a seventeen-date tour of Germany, and almost immediately every single concert became a sell-out. That in itself was pretty remarkable, just on the strength of two hits, but it showed the extent to which the band had won themselves fans.

They all believed in putting on a real show, and that was exactly what they did—and still do, of course. Even though the majority of the songs were unfamiliar to fans, since their first album was some months away, every number was almost drowned out by the screams from the audience.

They were a sensation, there was no doubt about it. In fact, they were all quite taken aback by the reception they were given all across the country. They'd been concentrating so hard on preparing the music and the show that the boys hadn't given a thought to everything else that might happen, all the mob scenes, and the crowds that followed them everywhere. In just a few days, in Germany, Justin said, "We usually have to take two or three bodyguards with us there." If one or other of the members of 'N Sync showed his face in public, there was instantly a crowd of girls around him. And while they loved the affection, it was overwhelming, coming out of the blue.

One of the strangest things that happened on the tour was running into the Spice Girls. That was something they'd never expected. The Spice Girls, really, had ignited the new wave of pop music and were already megastars. Not who 'N Sync would have expected to encounter in a German airport. But that was exactly what happened.

"They didn't have security and we didn't have security," Chris remembered. "We met them in the airport and we just sat down and talked with them. People were walking right by us."

JC said, "We recognized them from the video. We recognized Scary Spice's (Mel B) hair. They were still so new with it, like us. We told them, 'We're going to record a really cool song!'"

They already had, but with "Tearin' Up My Heart" still tearin' up the charts around Europe, there was no hurry to release it. The seventeen dates the band played in Germany let them know what they'd be in for once the whole album came out and people truly became familiar with their music. Essentially, everything would be mental, completely insane, once they started touring properly, and they needed to be mentally prepared for that.

By the standards they'd soon have to get used to, seventeen dates on the road was a mini-tour, a chance for them to find their feet and really break in the stage act, to judge what worked and what didn't, and maybe start a couple of new routines if necessary. It also introduced them to the rigors they'd be undergoing, traveling all the time, catching naps as they went or in hotel rooms, facing the press or television every day, and still being completely psyched up to perform every night. It was grueling, even for veterans, never mind newcomers, but 'N Sync took to it all like ducks to water. The energy of a crowd fed them, made them happy; there was nothing to compare with it.

They very quickly came up with two rituals to be performed faithfully before every show. The first was a quick game of hackey sack among the band members, to loosen them up and get them laughing.

"On tours we always play hackey sack before a show," Lance said. "We have to delay the show sometimes, because we're not very good."

"The hackey sack thing started off as like a joke," Justin explained. "But, it became this superstitious thing towards the middle of our tour. We're all like, 'We can't go onstage until we make this hackey.' "

But it's not the most important, or even the final, ritual the fivesome undertake before they roar onto the stage. That one comes when the five of them get together with their road crew, and pray. "Without praying, we wouldn't dare to take a step on the stage," they all agreed. For every member of 'N Sync, faith is very important. While they wouldn't try to impose their beliefs on anyone else, they're all very strong in their convictions about God and religion, and this is vital to them, a focus of energy before they begin to perform, and a reflection on exactly *why* they're doing it.

As soon as that was finished, they were psyched up for those appearances on the German stages. While these were the first chances audiences had to watch them perform live, in the flesh, their faces were already familiar from the endless photo shoots and articles—and also from the videos for the two singles, which had been aired often on Viva!, Germany's version of MTV, as well as MTV Europe.

What viewing audiences thought they saw and the reality behind the shoots proved to be quite different, however. The video for "I Want You Back" seemed to show the guys on a New York street. But that wasn't New York at all. It was actually Orlando, Florida—or at least a soundstage there. It was remarkable that it truly looked and felt like Manhattan. Even more remarkable, in these days of big budgets and endless shoots, was the fact that the filming was all done in twenty-four hours. Chris, Joey, JC, Lance, and Justin (as well as the crew) all worked straight through, from seven A.M. one morning to seven A.M. the next, the only breaks coming as the next shots were set up.

When they sat down with Johnny Wright and Lou Pearlman to watch the finished product, however, no one was quite satisfied. It had the look, there was no doubt about that, but it was missing a certain something—it could have been anybody; there was no sense of who 'N Sync really were. The solution was to add something that made them come alive. The idea of showing them playing basketball was Justin's suggestion, since he's the one who loves the game so much (and has some slick moves, as you can see from the video), and the others agreed. With a basketball court already there, and Justin having a round ball handy, they were ready to shoot the remaining footage very quickly.

While they were warming up, and in the footage that

didn't get used, it was Justin who was showing all the energy—and not just because he's the youngest. Still, it's not surprising, since he really keeps himself in shape, doing up to two hundred push-ups every day—even finding time when the band is on the road.

The video for "Tearin' Up My Heart" was, understandably, completely different. The only similarity is that, like its predecessor, it was shot in Orlando. This one took two days to film, still pretty quick by many standards. It presented the band in the studio, singing and dancing, rehearsing, and just plain goofing on each other. Justin and JC were more prepared for this type of taping than the others, given their extensive experience with television on *The Mickey Mouse Club*.

Both video shoots were tremendous learning experiences for the guys. For Chris, Joey, and Lance, they had their first opportunity to see themselves on TV, and to learn what kind of things—expressions and movements—worked, and what didn't. It was another way to become more professional, and to hone their presentation. JC and Justin were veterans, but this was them into their own gig, and that made it all the more vital that everything should go right.

It was hard work, there was no doubt about that. The end product might have looked straightforward and glamorous, but for every minute of footage there were hours and hours of work. Shots had to be set up, executed, then set up again and filmed from a different angle. There was take after take after take, looking for that perfect moment. And in between, for the guys, came endless waiting—something they'd be getting used to on the road.

In the end, it was all worthwhile. When they sat down and viewed the final cut of the video, they were happy with what they saw. There was no trace of the boredom or the tiredness they'd often felt during those two days. Instead it was vital, alive, sometimes funny—it was *them*. And everyone seemed to agree, as the videos went into heavy rotation in Germany and other countries on the European continent.

That first German tour gave 'N Sync their first taste of bus travel. This wasn't like going Greyhound; it was more like a massive camper, with room enough for all five guys to live and sleep. There was a refrigerator, microwave, and plenty of food and drink. Beds were set up, bunk-style, at the rear of the bus. There was a bathroom, with a shower and plenty of hot water. Everything was air-conditioned. And it wouldn't have been complete without a killer stereo system, a television, VCR . . . and a PlayStation for the guys to entertain themselves and challenge each other at games. With so much to occupy themselves, you might have thought the guys would have had a blast. And they did. But being so tightly confined (it might have felt like home, but it was still a bus) became wearing after a while.

Still, it was something they'd have to get used to. In May 1997, their debut album was set for release all over Europe, with a full-on tour to back it up, taking them all across the continent. With the singles having performed so well, there was great expectation that the album would fly out of the stores, and that the tour would make the band into a massive attraction.

Ahead of it all came the media blitz. Given the success they'd had, everybody wanted to talk to 'N Sync, and the guys were more than happy to oblige. So they found themselves flying from European capital to European capital, but without the time or freedom to really enjoy any of the cities, as they sat in rooms and answered question posed by journalists, or found themselves being shunted to locations for photo shoots. It was all wonderful, being the center of attention, but it wasn't their real aim. The boys were all eager for the tour to begin, so they could do what they did best—entertain.

FROM TINY ACORNS

Finally, May 26 arrived, and all the waiting was over for Lance, JC, Chris, Justin, and Joey. But they needn't have worried. Even before its release date, the album was a massive hit in Germany. The advance orders for *'N Sync* totaled 250,000—a huge amount for a debut album by anyone. Given the way sales in Germany worked, that meant they already had a gold record for the disc before anyone could actually buy a copy of it. It entered the chart at number twenty-two, then rose the following week all the way to Number One, the first Number One the band had enjoyed anywhere. According to their label, copies of *'N Sync* were leaving German record stores at the rate of 20,000 a day—the kind of figures to make any band feel happy.

It wasn't only Germany that couldn't get enough of 'N Sync. The album climbed to number five in both Sweden and Switzerland, and it made the top ten in Holland, Austria, and Hungary—all countries where the singles had done very well.

Of course, there were those who resented the success of any band, and were quick to write 'N Sync off as clones of the Backstreet Boys. But, as Lance pointed out, "In the beginning they also compared BSB to Take That. But they've figured out that we are not just a BSB clone."

And, Chris observed, "It happens. We just try not to dwell on it. Comparisons happen. We try to be our own group."

Quite obviously, they succeeded in a big way as the records continued to sell, and the massive European trek began. The German tour had been a taster, an introduction. This was the full spectacle, with the boys backed by a seven-piece band, performing all the material from *'N Sync* plus some other songs that no one had heard before.

It was all singing and all dancing. Even the ballads saw a lot of choreography and movement. That was the signature the boys gave to the music, the extra bit. The singing would have been fine all by itself, but they wanted to do what the Germans called "*mach schau*" and give the show a visual as well as an aural element.

A lot of rehearsal went before this tour, the first time they'd played on a stage with live musicians. They auditioned plenty of people for the job, but ended up mostly recruiting friends from Florida, people they'd known for quite a while and felt comfortable with. It was even more testament to all the talent in the area, working at the theme parks, clubs, and studios. Of course, there were constant adjustments to be made when they were on the road. The boys had worked with a couple of different choreographers putting the show together, perfecting all the movements, but if they felt something wasn't working right when they were on stage, they weren't above making changes and working out their own new routines.

That, of course, meant even more rehearsal, working with the band, and the only time they could find for it was early in the morning, long before most people were up, and before 'N Sync were due to meet the press, photographers, and radio people of whatever city they were in that particular day. It stretched them even tighter, but they didn't mind. This was their big break and they wanted everything to be absolutely *perfect*.

In the eyes of the audiences, there wasn't a note or a single movement out of place. The boys conquered Europe country by country. Each night the band was exhausted, but happy.

"We tour so hard," Justin said while it was all going on. "We've toured for a month straight, city after city, and we'd get maybe two days off the entire tour. I had never experienced touring to the point that you started losing weight!"

Lance was simply ecstatic with the way everything was happening. "Our success in Germany is sensational," he said. "It's breaking all records in Europe." And there was no doubt that they all thought it made those months rehearsing into the middle of the night, with nothing immediate in sight, worthwhile. Florida was a long way away, and they'd shown that dreams really could come true.

The album Europeans could buy was quite different from the version Americans would be flocking to purchase a year later. The name—'N Sync—was the same, the package looked the same, but there were quite a few changes in the content. "I Just Wanna Be With You," "I Drive Myself Crazy," "God Must Have Spent a Little More Time on You," and their cover of Bread's "Everything I Own" were all missing, replaced by "Riddle," "Best of My Life," "Together Again," "Forever Young," and a cover of the Boston song, "More Than a Feeling." In other words, the European CD was not only quite different to listen to, it was also one track longer.

Perhaps the strangest choice was to cover "More Than a Feeling." Back in the Seventies, Boston had been a big band for a while, with a melodic hard-rock style behind some very high lead vocals. The song had been written by the band's leader and guitarist, Tom Scholz. In September 1976, it had been a number five hit in America (and number twenty-two in England, incidentally), taken from Boston's debut album, which sold six million copies—an immense amount for that time. The song still crops up regularly on the classic rock stations. Of course, one thing 'N Sync wasn't and never pretended to be was a rock band. They were more interested in the vocal qualities and the harmonies that were inside the song, and they gave it much more of a ballad feel, with slower beats per minute than the original, finding the emotion that Boston's version had hidden under layers of guitars. The boys showed that underneath all the rock there was actually a very pretty song. It was part of the additional recording they ended up doing after their first German tour, this one recorded in Holland, with Jaap Eggermont at the producer's desk

"Forever Young" and "Together Again" weren't cover songs, although there were very well-known tunes with those titles. The former was one that the boys really loved, and still perform, in part because of its very inspirational message about persevering against all the odds—something they did themselves in the early days. Like "More Than a Feeling," it was a product of those European sessions after the first tour, designed to lend a slightly more Continental spin to the album, leaving it slightly less American and more international. This one was actually produced in Berlin, Germany, by Joern-Uwe Frankenkrog-Peterson and Frank Busch, and was written by Nemo Frankenkrog-Peterson, Jean Beauvoir, and Bettina Martinelli—the only work this team did with 'N Sync.

Veit Renn, who was responsible for quite a bit of the production work on 'N Sync, was behind the board for "Together Again," along with Gary Carolla. The song—which was definitely *not* the old fifties Buck Owens country hit—concerned itself with something the boys could definitely relate to, the problems of long-distance romance. Even though they hadn't left any girlfriends behind, their families were still in Florida, while they were thousands of miles away. Even though the band hadn't experienced that loneliness when they recorded their vocals—in Florida—they still managed to summon up the sense of aching and loss that only distance can bring.

"Riddle" was something altogether different, upbeat, bouncy, one of those "women are from Venus, men are from Mars" songs, as the boys try to understand what a girl is thinking (and, as everyone knows, trying to figure out the thought processes of the opposite sex is a lost cause). To be more specific, trying to figure out what the girl they're crushing on is thinking, just to make the task even harder. But it wasn't really a love song as such; it was quite humorous in both the writing and the singing. This was the third and last of the "European" batch of 'N Sync songs, produced once again by Veit Renn, although the actual final mixing of the track was done in Florida.

The final different track on the European version of the album was "Best of My Life," put together by BOOYA Music Productions (B.Artis, T. Cottura, and VD Toorn), who were also responsible for "Here We Go," which would be the boys' third single. The song's title was definitely misleading. While it sounded happy, it was actually a reflection on a wonderful relationship, on all the good times, after the breakup had happened, a painful breakup the singer hadn't wanted at all. The times he'd spent with the girl, he decided, had been the best of his life.

Those were the songs that made the European version of 'N Sync—actually, the version released all over the world—different from the American version that would follow in 1998. Obviously, for any serious fan of Justin,

Chris, Joey, Lance, and JC, it's a necessary purchase—where else are you going to be able to hear those songs? If you should decide it's something you really can't live without, you'd better be aware that's it's going to cost you quite a bit—about twice as much as you'd pay for an American CD. Those five tracks might be worth the extra money, though . . . they're all great.

To coincide with the album, a new single arrived on the scene, as the boys released "Here We Go," which just shot up the charts all across the Continent, rising to number eight in Germany, firmly consolidating their success. There was going to be no stopping 'N Sync now—they were on a roll, and they were going with it.

The video for the song was quite a spectacle, a basketball game of 'N Sync taking on the Austrian national youth basketball team—quite a contest. It was shot in the gym at the American International School in Vienna, and to an extent was a real exhibition game, given that it was impossible to really choreograph the passes and slam dunks.

The idea for the video came, not too surprisingly, from Justin, since it gave him the chance to live out his fantasy of being a pro basketball player.

"When we are at home in Orlando, JC, Chris, and I are practicing almost every day in our backyard, where we have a real basketball court. Now we can show our fans what we can do on our court," he said.

The three of them might have spent a lot of time shooting hoops, but Joey and Lance weren't big-time ball players, which meant, as Chris explained, that "JC, Justin, and I had to play with double effort."

The video was a treat for the fans in more way than one. One hundred female fans were on the set, sitting on the bleachers, and another six were selected to play cheerleaders, with the pom-poms and red skirts, cheering as the boys took the court and performed an elaborate warm-up routine. While "Here We Go" blasted through the speakers, Lance, Justin, Chris, Joey, and JC danced, jumped, and did somersaults.

Their opponents were no slouches—this was, after all, a national team, and in the real game, the Austrians quickly took the lead, although 'N Sync managed to claw their way back. The real turning point came when Chris made a three-point basket from center court. The fans were caught up in the event, cheering the band on . . . and in the end, it was 'N Sync who emerged as the victors.

To crown it all there was a party (with some of the footage making it into the video) that the band hosted for its fans who'd come down, and also their opponents, who'd played well and given their all to try and beat the boys. It was an ideal, fun way to make a video. Not only did they get to play a sport that the majority of the guys loved, they were able to get close to a group of fans. There was plenty of exercise . . . and there was also a very sweet victory over a good team. Life didn't get much better than that, really.

When their long trek through Europe was finally over, 'N Sync had won millions of hearts. Pop magazines were falling over themselves to name them as the best newcomers of 1997, even though the year was barely half over. It couldn't have gone any better, or been any sweeter, if it had been planned down to the last detail. For the guys, it was a vindication that the faith they'd had in themselves and their abilities was quite justified. And for Lou Pearlman and Johnny Wright, it proved that their instincts for perfect pop were still very finely honed.

One thing that had been changing slowly was the look of the guys themselves. The five piece that had gone to Europe in 1996 had been pretty cleancut. Joey had had flat hair then, his bangs cut straight and high on his forehead. Lance looked very young, his hair pale blond and soft. Joey's hair was combed straight back. Chris had short hair that he usually hid under baseball caps and long sideburns. Justin's hair was short, quite conservative and jock-ish.

It was amazing what a few months' exposure to the fashions and styles of Europe had done to the band. They'd seen how cool some of the things were over there, and taken on a mix and match of European and American clothes and haircuts. Joey still wore his hair combed back, but now the sides were cut really short, and he'd grown a goatee. He'd also discovered a taste for some truly outlandish and garish clothes. JC had grown out his hair a little, and he no longer had bangs. Instead it was greased up a little, and piled higher on his head, giving his face a very Fifties, movie star look, and emphasizing his strong, square chin. Gone was the functional windbreaker, and in its place was something more casual: baggy jeans, and a shirt over a T-shirt. Lance had cropped and spiked his blond hair, and the Southern boy had emerged from his shell into some very fashionable threads. Justin's hair was bleached now, with some highlights that were almost white. Instead of sweatshirts and khakis, he too was wearing baggy clothes and polo shirts.

The one who'd undergone the biggest change, however, was Chris. His hair had grown way out, and the baseball caps were something of the past. His hair was shaggy and wild, the hair dark. His sideburns were thicker, and he was sporting a small goatee. The picture on the back of the album showed him dressed all in black, wearing a Seventies style leather jacket, black T-shirt, and jeans. He looked edgy, maybe even a little bit dangerous, although he wasn't really.

What it all meant was that each of the boys had grown into his own style. Lance was fashionable but still a little conservative, JC casual, Justin tidy, experimenting a little bit, Joey loud, and Chris dark. It was something they probably needed to do, a chance to find themselves, and also create a blend that worked. When they'd left the

States they were still unformed in a number of ways. Time abroad and on the road had altered all that. The relative freedom they'd had, to dress as they wanted, to make changes in hair and styles, brought them home again with the kind of flair that was generally absent in Orlando.

Coming home after the tour was certainly an interesting experience for them all. All through Europe they'd been surrounded by screaming fans, playing shows in big halls to massive crowds. They'd become *stars*, and that meant they'd been treated differently. As soon as the 747 began its journey across the Atlantic, however, it was altogether a different story. Maybe their album had hit number one. Maybe their cases were full of awards. Maybe they had gold records and impressive sales figures. Once they touched down on American soil, though, that didn't mean a thing. They were just five more young guys that no one outside their families and friends had ever heard of.

It was a jolt, to be sure. But the reality check was also welcome. It gave them the chance to walk around without being mobbed, to do the everyday things—go to the store, catch a movie—without bodyguards or precautions. It served to remind them all that they were real people, not figures up on a stage. If they'd started to walk on air in Europe, this brought them quickly back to earth.

"We consider it lucky that we hit in Europe and got so huge but remained unknown in the States," Justin said. "It gave us the chance to sit back and digest what was happening as it happened. We might have gotten crazy about it, but then we'd come home and it was like a reality check. We certainly didn't expect things to go as they did in Europe. We hope to have half as much success in the U.S."

That time was still a little way off, however. Pop music had broken big in the America, thanks to the twin phenomena known as the Spice Girls and Hanson, both of whom were selling millions of copies of their albums. The idea of bands that appealed primarily to teenagers was no longer a bad thing. People had come to realize that teens didn't just automatically like the music their older brothers and sisters were listening to—particularly if that happened to be angst-filled alternative. Once they were given the option of something warmer, more upbeat, and sunnier, they jumped on it. And why shouldn't they? It was something they could truly call their own, which had been missing for too many years.

However, was America in 1997 ready for boy bands? The answer seemed to be not really. The ones who'd hit first—Take That, East 17, and Boyzone—had made absolutely no impact in the U.S. Part of that was timing, but it was also the music, which just didn't appeal to American teens the way it did to Europeans.

Even the Backstreet Boys hadn't been able to make a dent in the American market when they began in 1994. Europe—well, the entire rest of the world, really—had been the place to embrace them with open arms. But in 1997 they decided to bring it all back home again, and in July released the single "Quit Playing Games (With My Heart)." The signal that there'd been a major shift of attitude came when MTV started playing the video in heavy rotation. Suddenly, BSB were big news. Showing up for a CD signing at Tower Records in Torrance, California, there were several *hundred* girls waiting for them—a replay of what they, and 'N Sync, had experienced in Europe. It was beginning to seem very much as if pop music was making its way back to the States, and that a lot of fans were very pleased about that. It gave them a music of their own, something a lot of older siblings hated—even better—but which parents could tolerate, since it wasn't extreme. There were even songs that parents could *like*. The concerts by these bands might have been filled with screaming from the fans, but at least they were safe, and actually quite wholesome.

The surest sign came when BSB's single entered the *Billboard* chart at number twenty-four, much higher than anyone could have anticipated. America was finally understanding what Europe had known for years, that boy bands could be a lot of fun.

That still didn't mean that 'N Sync was ready to unleash its music on America. What they really needed was to be firmly established in Europe first. They'd had three wicked hit singles and a massive album, and done one major tour. All of those were tremendous achievements, to be sure, but they needed some consolidation before coming home to show everyone there what they could do.

And there were other demands on their time. Not only had the record done well across the continent of Europe, but Britain had caught onto them, and so had Asia. The fire that was 'N Sync was spreading like crazy, all across the globe. The time they had at home was just long enough to decompress, catch up on laundry, and feel like human beings again. Then it was time to go back on the road. In this case, though, it wouldn't be a concert tour. This was promotion, and it would find them getting a lot of stamps in their passports.

To say that the world was rapidly becoming their oyster was something of an understatement. London was a knockout, and welcomed them as they performed on a couple of television shows, promoting "Here We Go." It would have been impossible to have been so close without hitting other European countries, so they found themselves back in what had become their home away from home—Germany—appearing on Viva! and radio stations, before heading off to the Far East.

That was unlike anything that Chris, Justin, Lance, JC, or Joey had ever seen before. The fans were every bit as avid as their European counterparts—but a lot more polite. In Germany, all over, they'd been mobbed, hounded for autographs. In Spain the fans had gotten quite phys-

ical with them, trying to tear of their clothes and pull at
their hair (this was something other bands had noted, too,
on their travels). But in the East, politeness ruled. The
fans still wanted autographs, but they waited, and asked
for them, followed by profuse thanks, as if they boys had
done them a huge favor. In Manila, Tokyo, Singapore, it
was the same, and something that was very much appreciated. And finally it was on to Australia, to Sydney,
which gave them a chance to have a glance at life Down
Under—which wasn't too different from America, really.
With one difference. They already knew, and loved, 'N
Sync.

Coming back from that whirlwind round-the-world
trip gave the boys even more of a shock. It was like
having been in space, orbiting the world, and then suddenly arriving back on earth again. Instead of room service or fast food, now it was mom's cooking, and sleeping
in the rooms they'd inhabited for years (well, for most
of them). It was Florida sunshine and heat, a chance to
go to the beach.

It was also a chance to spend some of the money
they'd earned. While they'd been selling albums and singles and touring, the money had been mounting up. But
there'd been absolutely no chance to spend it, no time.
Now they were home again, with the money in their ac-
counts, most of the boys felt as if they deserved something, some way of acknowledging all they'd achieved.
For three of them, that meant buying the cars of their
dreams. Joey went shopping for an Acura, and drove
home with a lovely Acura SLX. JC wanted something
more rugged, that could get him away into the country,
and he quickly settled on a vehicle that was perfect for
him—a Jeep. And Justin found his perfect transporta-
tion—a Mercedes van. Needless to say, they were all
fitted with top-of-the-range stereo systems with some
kickin' bass. While neither Chris nor Lance bought cars—
and still don't own them—there were plenty of good

times to be had by everybody just cruising in the sunshine with some jams playing, enjoying the freedom of not having to be awake early, or keeping an endless series of appointments.

The downtime was necessary, because early in 1998 they'd be back in Europe, touring again. The truth was, Europe couldn't get enough of the boys. Demand for concerts was high. They would be playing huge halls this time around, some of the biggest around, and tickets were selling out at an unheard-of pace—they sold out one arena in less than half an hour!

A new tour meant some new choreography, as well as some new songs, including a cover of something very close to Joey's heart—a real old doo-wop song, "The Lion Sleeps Tonight" (also known as "Wimoweh" in its original Zulu form), which had been a hit for the Tokens in 1961. Joey's father, of course, had been a doo-wop singer himself, and so this was something of a tribute to him.

So while they were back home, it wasn't all play. There was plenty of work to be put into a new stage show, lots of rehearsal time. But there was also something more. Plans were being discussed for the release of 'N Sync's album in America in the late spring. And that meant thinking about tours, booking some television, and letting the press know all about the newest sensations.

None of that was the band's job, but they needed to be aware of what would be happening—after all, it would involve them. And, after the success they'd enjoyed abroad, they desperately wanted to do well at home.

TO MIGHTY OAKS

Europe was everything they could have hoped. The boys put on a big show, sang plenty of songs, and enjoyed themselves on stage. Joey got to meet up again with someone he'd become close to—Lene Crawford Nystrom, the singer of the Swedish band Aqua.

They'd originally met in October 1997 at the Pepsi Pop Festival in Rotterdam, Holland, and she was the one who made the running, not him!

"I had a crush on him from first sight!" she admitted. The two bands got to know each other, and Joey and Lene paired off. She visited him in Orlando, and when 'N Sync hit Europe again on the tour trail, Lene was at some of the shows—and was also seen with Joey afterward.

"Lene is very attractive and sexy and I love her sense of humor," he said. "She's spontaneous—and I like a woman with a female look."

Was it serious? Well, she was telling people that "I'm really in love with one of 'N Sync, but I won't make trouble for the boys, they have many female fans." In other words, she was quite serious about him—but she was going to keep herself, and whatever relationship they had, very much in the background.

And how did Joey feel about having a babe like that after him?

"I like Lene for a girlfriend, but our careers don't let us—there's not enough time to build a strong relationship."

Which has certainly been quite true, as the boys tore through Europe, and Aqua also had to deal with plenty of international stardom themselves. Whatever they shared—and possibly still share—was something of a victim of their respective successes.

It's the nearest any of the guys had come to the love thang since the band had taken off, and that much had only been possible because Lene knew the kind of pressure Joey was living under, and all the demands on his time. Also, living in a similar world, she was able to use her free time to fly around to 'N Sync shows.

Through January and February, the 'N Sync bus ate up the miles on the autobahns and motorways of Europe. For all the boys saw of them, one city might as well have been another. There was time to sleep, rehearse, eat, meet the press, and then get all the energy out of their systems every night with a show in front of thousands of screaming fans. And when it was all over, there was finally the chance to sit in the Florida sun again, some peace and quiet. But if they were lucky, this would be the very last time they'd be anonymous at home. As soon as they'd had a chance to recharge their batteries, the assault on America was about to begin in earnest.

Actually, it had already begun. The single had appeared late in February, and, just as it had in Europe, "I Want You Back" exploded into national consciousness. There was no shortage of airplay for the record, and MTV put the video into heavy rotation. Within a couple of weeks, it had debuted on the *Billboard* Hot 100, showing that, finally, it was time for the boys to come home and claim their place.

The single did more than merely hit the charts—it kept rising and rising, all the way to number thirteen. Even then, it didn't seem to want to go away, hanging around for a solid, and quite unbelievable, six months. In the process it sold enough copies—more than half a million—to go gold. Which meant that it was a pretty impressive debut.

"I heard the song on the radio on *Casey's Top 40*," Lance laughed, "and it was weird, because we all grew up listening to Casey Kasem. It sounded so good!" He had every right to be happy. After their time away, 'N Sync were finally proving they could do it at home, too. But they'd all known from the start that this would be the song to do it.

"When we first heard this song with its groove, and the heavy beat behind it, we knew it was a hit," JC said.

The single preceded the album by a month, so it was already in the charts when *'N Sync* was released, on RCA, part of the international BMG group, right at the end of March. But even though they had a hit, not a lot of people in America knew them. During the course of April they did their best to change that, traveling all over the country, and meeting—or so it seemed—as many of the population as they possibly could.

They were used to these promotional trips by now, but this was almost the first time they'd jetted from city to city and remained in the same country! The planes took them from New York to California, their native Florida, into the Midwest, the Northwest, all over, working hard to promote the album, to talk and sing on radio shows, and—the biggest thrill of all for their new fans—to do plenty of CD signings in record stores. They worked with the big chains, Tower, Sam Goody, and others, and wrote their names literally thousands of times over the course of a month, sending a lot of people home very happy.

And the guys were happy to go directly to the fans. After all, they were the ones who were spending their money on the records, the ones who were making it all into a hit. And they were the ones, the band hoped, who'd be coming out to see them when they began touring in the U.S. The bottom line was that the fans were the most important thing, and if it made them feel good, then the boys were more than happy to be doing it.

Certainly, the fans all seemed happy with them. Copies of the album just flew out of the stores, and the disc vaulted straight into the *Billboard* album charts, which it would continue to climb through the year, all the way to number three. By the end of 1998 it had spent a truly staggering thirty-eight weeks on the chart, and was still at its peak of number three, with more than four million copies sold—quadruple platinum. Not at all bad for a first album.

The record kicked off, of course, with the great pop of "Tearin' Up My Heart." With Justin singing lead on the Max Martin/Kristian Lundin tune, produced by Lundin at Denniz Pop's Cheiron Studios in Stockholm, Sweden, the song had major hit written all over it. The bass kicked deep like any good dance track should, the chorus was so catchy that you couldn't help singing it (particularly with that xylophone line hovering above it), and the harmonies that came on full force in the second verse gave warning that the boys were a real force. The video, set around a photo shoot for the boys, also gave them the chance to indulge some fantasy ninja skills and kickboxing poses, as part of it required them to jump off a balcony in a warehouse (there was a big mattress to land on). While stylish, even a quick viewing made it apparent that it was an old video, actually filmed in the spring of 1997. Everyone looked different—Chris didn't have his cornrows, Joey was beardless, JC's hair was still flat, and Lance looked incredibly well-groomed. But the action and continual movement carried it all, and made it well worth seeing.

Full Force were responsible for "I Just Wanna Be With You," the instrumental tracks recorded in New York, before adding the vocals at the boys' home of Trans Continental Studios in Orlando. This track, like everything Full Force handled, definitely had da funk under the lovely harmonies. The instrumental track contained a sample of Sly and the Family Stone's "Family Affair" (one of the funkiest songs ever written). It was a small step to R&B for the guys, while still keeping one foot firmly in their pop roots. The vocal arrangement was actually quite complex, but the guys handled it easily and gracefully.

"Here We Go" had already emerged as a favorite of the live set. It bounced in a real Euro-dance song. Propelled by the band, it gave full rein to the harmonies, while giving plenty of opportunity for an audience to chant along on the title. It was easy to see why a B-ball video was the perfect setting for this. It would never be right as a single, but it worked well in the context of an album, and there was no doubt it would be able to get people up and moving.

Producer Veit Renn co-wrote "For the Girl Who has Everything" with Jolyon Skinner, and this was a real full step into Babyface style R&B, with Justin's lead vocal standing out (actually, some of his vocal were recorded in Munich, Germany, although most of the track was laid down in Florida). Justin handled the verses, sounding much older than his years, with the rest of the boys coming in on the chorus—with some subtle really high harmony from Chris. By the second verse, the band was in full effect. It was as if Babyface had sat down with Boyz II Men to create a gorgeous slow jam—and it worked perfectly. With Renn himself playing guitar, it was soft, like walking on a plush carpet—you felt as if you were actually walking on air as the track progressed. In many ways, a song and arrangement like this helped 'N Sync really shine even more than their pop material. It offered an alert that there was really much more going on here than them just being top popsters; they could also be slow, sexy, and superb. The song was released as a European single, and a video made to accompany it, two stories that intertwined at the end. The boys found themselves shipwrecked on a desert island. Marooned along with them was a girl's trunk. In it was a camera and a bottle. They took a picture of themselves, put it in the bottle, and tossed it out to see. It was found in New York by a bored rich girl who had everything but love (the trunk was also supposed to have been hers, but quite how that was managed was never explained). It was a message song—you might have everything you could want materially, but without love, it means very little.

That led into the wonderful "God Must Have Spent a Little More Time on You," as romantic a ballad as anyone was going to find anywhere, written and produced by Carl Sturken and Evan Rogers, with the basic tracks recorded in Bronxville, N.Y., at the Loft, the vocals in Orlando, and the string at the famous Electric Lady Studios in New York City. This was a song that, as 1998 ended, would prove so popular and so requested, even as an album track, that it would climb the *Billboard* singles chart—which was pretty good going, indeed. It was a gorgeous love song, a song about *falling* in love, a fairly spare arrangement that really allowed the boys' voices to shine, with a simple melody that really worked. Each of the guys got his solo turn in front of the microphone. It was soulful, soft, and yes, even spiritual, and it was definitely Justin's favorite on the album. The video took a slightly different tack from the obvious—a mother's love for her son, and images of him growing, playing baseball, studying, and finally going off to serve in World War II. After no word, she's scared when she opens the door to find a man in uniform—but soon discovers it's her son, home safe and sound. It was sentimental, but then the song was sentimental, and unabashedly romantic.

Veit Renn was back behind the boards for "You Got It," with everything recorded at Orlando's Parc Studios. This was straight Eurofunk, where the voices got a real harmony workout, particularly in the upper registers, as the song zipped along. It was tricky, with lots of small vocal flourishes to test the guys, and in some ways it actually recalled the Bee Gees, with a midsection that was heavily influenced by some of the vocal groups of the Fifties, like the Four Freshman. So, as a showcase for what they could really do, it was superb.

"I Need Love" was a Gary Carolla composition and production, also recorded at Parc Studios. It was pure Nineties pop (with quite a few Eighties touches), carried by the voices over a buzzing bass synth. It was the little touches in the arrangements in the arrangement that were really retro, not to the mention the galloping rhythm—if this had come out in 1983 as a single it would have been totally massive, and 'N Sync would have been bigger than Culture Club. As an homage to an era, it worked brilliantly. Of course, it also worked pretty neatly on its own terms, too. . . .

Then came *the* song, "I Want You Back," with its introduction leading into those harmonies, then that funky piano line. It was Denniz Pop and Max Martin magic (Pop would sadly pass away in September 1998). Mid-paced, it used the harmonies to full effect, with a spare arrangement that was Pop's hallmark, a hip-hop beat behind the voices, particularly Justin's lead. One listen was all you needed to know this would be huge. That bassline had more hooks than ten fishing poles, and the churchy bridge exploded into glorious harmonies from the boys. This was the song that had broken them everywhere, the one that had torn up the charts all over the world; it was simply irresistible. There was everything going for it, particularly when you added in the video.

But even on the radio, it was perfect, the absolute epit-
ome of Nineties pop music. The American video, as
everyone knows, showed what the guys were like, playing hoops, foosball, pool, generally enjoying themselves,
and driving round in JC's convertible after he'd been
dumped by his girlfriend. The female dancers (shot on
the same street scene as the boys) never made it to the
final cut—and, really, they weren't missed.

However, there had been an earlier, very different, version of the video made and used when the song was a
hit in Europe. Why wasn't it just recycled in America?
Well, by then it was a year old, and the guys all looked
very different. Chris had a pretty slick haircut, as did
Joey, and Justin really did look about fifteen. In a short
time, they'd all grown a great deal, in every way. The
people on that video still existed, but it wouldn't have
done them any kind of justice. Set on some kind of in-
terplanetary base, it was about a girl who couldn't quite
manage to materialize (which gave it some humor), while
the guys sang and danced the song—although the choreography was nowhere near as good as that used in the
American video. If you want a sneak peek at what the
boys used to be like, though, check it out. It's available
on *'N Sync 'N The Mix: The Official Home Video*.

There was probably only one way to follow that, and
it was with some classic mellow pop, in the form of the
old Bread hit, "Everything I Own," which had been
written by David Gates, and was a major soft-rock hit for
the band in the early 1970s. The Full Force production,
recorded in New York and Orlando, put a slightly different spin on things, however. Instead of a fairly straight
reading of the original, after a straightforward opening,
it turned into a densely arranged R&B song. Probably it
seemed a little weird to anyone who'd grown up with
Bread's version, but to everyone else it made perfect
sense. Chris's falsetto was able to glide above the chords,
with the other guys offering a bed of harmonies. On the

bridge the boys were able to trade some vocal licks over the strings, then turn the chorus kind of funky, before a spoken-word part.

"I Drive Myself Crazy" was another Veit Renn production, with everything recorded at Trans Continental. Another slow jam, it leaned a bit toward that Babyface tip, with an aching, soft chorus. It could easily have stood as a single, and confirmed—if any confirmation was needed by this point—just how strong the 'N Sync harmonies really were. It deftly mixed R&B and pop, taking the best bits of both—the catchy chorus and the soulful vocals—and putting them in one lovely package. And when the harmonies really took over, going through a couple of key changes, the effect was pure magic.

Gary Carolla produced "Crazy for You" (no, crazy wasn't any kind of album subtext—just a coincidence) at Parc Studios in Orlando. It had that funk/metal line that brought in the vocals, and a truly killer chorus. But, compared to the rest of the material on the album, this was probably the weakest song. The separate parts worked individually, but somehow never quite seemed to hang together—and that little metal bit *really* didn't do justice to those amazing voices. Not that it was bad, by any means, just not up to the standard of the rest. Still, in the live shows it was a real workout number, one which always satisfied the crowds, and the boys did use it as an opportunity to let their guitarist show off his chops a little bit.

"Sailing" was another cover of a Seventies hit, this one having been written and performed by Christopher Cross. 'N Sync's version was produced by Veit Renn, who seemed to work really well with the guys, and bring out something special in them. This one opened with the those Fifties-style harmonies that had originally influenced the Beach Boys. The song, which was really about sailing, had a perfect Florida feel—what could have been more ideal for the boys?—over its simple guitar changes.

The arrangement really filled out from the original, using the great harmonies to full advantage, where the backgrounds were every bit as important as the lead. In some ways it might well have seemed the odd track out on the album, very different from anything else. It would appeal more to mom and dad than anyone buying the record, but it really was a beautiful piece of work, showing the range of the voices, and the harmonizing ability probably more than any other song on 'N Sync. There was a lot of subtlety, nothing in your face, four and a half minutes of gossamer loveliness.

But it was the final track, "Giddy Up," which was something really special, since it was the first 'N Sync composition, co-written with Veit Renn, who also produced the song, to make it onto disc. Like "Sailing," it had been recorded at The House of Hits, another studio in Orlando. Starting with the kind of scratches you'd get from old vinyl, it went straight into some serious funk, before sliding into some very sexy R&B over a hip-hop beat. The scratches appeared behind the chorus again. Given their vocal abilities, it was no surprise that the harmonies and backing vocals worked beautifully on the track. For the first song they'd had recorded, though, it was *very* mature and professional, definitely not the work of novices.

But that was true of the entire album. It was assured, intricate. And there was no way on earth it couldn't be a hit.

The CD actually held an extra few treats for anyone with a computer and a CD-ROM player. If you slipped it in, not only could you listen to the disc, but there was a whole enhanced side to the CD. So you got the band bio, the songs' lyrics (as well as full credits for the writing and producing), some very cool photos, and even some video footage. Plus, you could even hook up through the internet to America Online and catch what they had to say about the band—which was plenty, given that the guys would do two AOL chats during 1998. All of that made it a double gift, really, something everyone could happily deal with. Enhanced CDs were definitely the wave of the future, and using the technology was not only a cool idea, but it also gave people more of an introduction to the band, and made them much more than faceless voices—it gave them backgrounds and personalities, really bringing them to life.

If April had been busy criss-crossing the country and building up the air miles, it was merely setting the stage for May, when 'N Sync would headline their first performances in America. But these weren't just any performances. The shows in Minneapolis, Orlando, and New York, and other places—they did quite a few concerts for radio stations, including one in Anaheim, California, that drew many thousands—were very, very high profile, a chance for the guys to reach a lot of people very quickly, and to show just what they were like in concert.

Minnesota is the home to the largest mall in the U.S., the Mall of America, in Bloomington, just outside Minneapolis. If you think you've seen malls, you've seen nothing until you've been to this place. Call it a shopper's paradise or whatever you want, it dwarfs the places most people know as malls.

Outside this massive structure was the place where 'N Sync would make their real American debut. In a way, perhaps, it was fitting that such a massive band would do it by a place that was already in the record books for its size.

The album and the single were both performing tremendously, but, in all honesty, the guys had no idea what to expect. Would lots of people come to see them, or would they end up playing to thousands?

Part of the parking lot had been cleared, and a stage built for the show. The dressing room was under the stage, so the boys had absolutely no idea what was happening outside. It turned out that literally thousands of people were filling the area, eager to get a glimpse of 'N Sync, to hear and see what it was really all about.

"It was so funny because we were getting ready for the show under the lower level and we couldn't hear anything," was Justin's recollection. "We walked up and there was a line that security made going to the stage. There were about two or three hundred people and we saw people blocked into this section, and we found out later that there were six or seven thousand people. We were like, 'Wow!' We came on stage and it was just, raah!''

To be home, in their own country, and be greeted by crowds like that, felt like a real triumph. Europe and Asia had been wonderful, they'd taken the boys to their hearts, but success at home, that recognition, was important to them all. It really made them feel as if they'd arrived.

"We were hoping to [do well in America]," Lance said. "We didn't think it would come this fast! We owe it all to our fans!"

As a start, it was far more than they'd ever hoped. But, it turned out, this performance would be the tip of the iceberg. From Minneapolis, they jumped on a plane heading back to Orlando.

They were going to a weekend party. Not just any party, but one which would see them hitting the highest point yet of their career in terms of visibility. Walt Disney World was celebrating the opening of a new attraction at the theme park, Animal Kingdom, and 'N Sync were there to help inauguarate it. As part of the festivities, they would also be filming an *In Concert* special for the Disney Channel, to be screened a little later in the year.

It all began on Friday, as the boys got a personal and private tour of the new attraction. Of course, they were trailed by camera crews, eager to capture all the best moments and provide some candid footage of the guys as they enjoyed themselves. Then, as part of the build-up to the main event, they held a press conference in the Rainforest Cafe.

"We're doing this special," Joey said, "we're doing a show in New York soon."

"We're very excited about it," Lanced added.

They even ended things with an unaccompanied version of "I Drive Myself Crazy," which was on the 'N Sync album—everyone except Chris, who had a sore throat, and needed to nurse his voice, saving it for the main event the following day.

The press conference was followed by a brief interview for the Disney Channel. After that, they all finally got some time to themselves—and got to take their families on all the Disney World rides. It made for a very full day, and as evening came, they were happy to go back to their respective homes—which was something of a treat in itself—and catch up on sleep in their own beds.

Saturday was as crammed as Friday. First off they made their handprints in a Walk of Fame. The idea came from the Walk of Fame in Hollywood, California, outside Graumann's Chinese Theater. The Disney version captured the prints of those who'd been important in Disney productions, people like Robin Williams and Bette Midler.

After that came another press conference, not with the media this time, but with the people who really counted— the fans. At the Beauty and the Beast Amphitheater (being ferried there in a pair of classic convertibles, accompanied by Mickey and Minnie Mouse), they had a real chance to talk to their fans, and answer all manner of questions. It led to an impromptu performance, when one girl told the boys it was her friend's birthday. Immediately, the five launched into perfect harmony on a version of "Happy Birthday"—to a girl named Kayla, who will probably never forget the day as long as she lives.

The rest of the day was taken up with preparation for the concert. There were vocal warm-ups to be completed, wardrobe, sound checks, until, finally, it was show time.

And what a show it was! They played songs from the album, their version of "The Lion Sleeps Tonight," which had become a concert favorite for both band and fans, as well as covers of tunes by Michael Jackson and the Bee Gees (they planned to contribute a song to an upcoming Bee Gees tribute album). It might have been the most energetic stage performance they'd ever given, although, since they were always so hyper up there, it was difficult to be sure. One thing was certain, though—the choroegraphy was perfect, and the acrobatics and backflips of Justin, JC, and Joey had never looked better.

Just how good it was would become evident in the summer, when it was finally aired on television. As part of an *In Concert* series on the Disney Channel, 'N Sync found themselves up against some top names, people like LeAnn Rimes and Brandy. But it was 'N Sync who grabbed the attention—and the ratings, the highest of any of the series, so much so that the channel was forced to repeat it several times over the course of the summer to satisfy viewer requests.

For many, the television concert was their first exposure to the band. And a lot of the people who watched, again and again, became instant converts to the 'N Sync camp. In turn, they went out and bought the album, sending it even further up the charts.

You might say that the television special really broke them in America. They'd already made an impact, just through radio and MTV, but this show truly put them over the top. People, fans and newcomers alike, were able to put faces to the voices, and see just what kind of a spectacular show they put on, managing to do all the singing and dancing. It made them *real*. And, in turn, that brought them even more fans. After all, not only were they talented, but they were also amazingly cute. Justin, in particular, found himself singled out for fan attention. But each of the guys had their supporters who just loved them.

One other important thing the special did was silence, once and for all, all those critics who'd been dismissing them as BSB clones. Sure, they had the same management and came from the same city, and both bands had five singing members, but that was as far as it went. They were two completely different groups, and 'N Sync had firmly established their own identity now. People liked them for who *they* were and how *they* sounded, not for any similarity there might have been to anyone else.

Once they'd finished filming in Orlando, it was time to pack their bags and return to the airport. This time they were heading to the Northeast, to take on the Big Apple, New York City, for the first time.

Every year Z100, one of the major pop radio stations that had helped break a lot of acts who'd gone on to become huge, put on a concert. The money raised usually went to charity, and this was no exception, the proceeds being given to PAX, a non-profit organization dedicated to ending the violence caused by handguns.

The station had put together a remarkable bill this year—holding it at the legendary Radio City Music Hall, which was celebrating its one hundredth anniversary. Mariah Carey and Gloria Estefan were the headliners, which would have been enough to draw thousands. But on top of that came Paula Cole, Matchbox 20, Third Eye Blind, K-Ci and JoJo, and Olivia Newton-John. Last, but very far from least, came the newest stars. 'N Sync.

"We're thinking, 'Oh my God, we're at Radio City Music Hall,' " said Lance, adding that the show was remarkable because of the people they got to meet, "A lot of celebrities we grew up listening to. One of my favorites was Olivia Newton-John."

They always gave every show their all, but surrounded by so much talent, they gave everything a special push, and it was noticed. A review in *Billboard* singled out the ''performance by 'N Sync, who danced and sang like banshees amid throngs of mesmerized and screaming girls.''

In reality, the whole 'N Sync machine was just warming up with these shows. In June they were really getting into gear, and back on the type of schedule the band had been used to in Europe. The whole of summer was the season for radio stations to put on big outdoor concerts, and the band was booked into their share of those, all over the country, mixing them with promotional appearance at stores, everywhere that seemed suitable. It brought them face-to-face with the fans, and kept alive just who they were doing all this for.

One place they'd never been was Canada, which was odd, given that their records had been on sale there long before they'd reached America, and they'd sold very well. They owed the fans, all those who'd made their discs into hits in Canada, and they repaid the debt in July, 1988, as they spent most of the month there, playing shows and doing endless promotion, traveling back and forth between the East and West coasts.

But they all knew that was how you did things. Someone who buys a CD has the music. Someone who'd seen them in concert not only had the music, they also had the memories, which could last a lot longer, and be a lot stronger. It forged a bond. And since they loved to perform, that was perfect. Canada, like everywhere, received them with open arms, as each show sold out, and their television appearances found ratings going through the roof.

That was July. August found them back in the U.S. touring the country on a very grass-roots level. They'd played more than their share of stadiums and arenas around the world—including America—and they had a Top Ten album and a huge hit single. But that didn't mean they could rest on their laurels. To a lot of people, 'N Sync was still nothing more than a name. And the best way to win new fans, or convert those who hadn't really cared before, was perform for them. Arena concerts were fine, and they had the fans who'd come and fill the place. But the way to reach all those other people was to go to them, and that was exactly the strategy the band pursued.

"We did a theme park tour in August, you know, Six Flags and state fairs," said Lance. That was where the families went, kids and parents together. Along with the rides, they wanted entertainment, and the band were well seasoned as entertainers by now. They could put on an impressive show for everybody, just knocking them out with the acrobatic dancing and their wonderful harmonies, so that they'd want to go home and buy their records.

The theme parks and state fairs were two places to catch people, but perhaps the best idea of all was to have 'N Sync performing in malls. It might have seemed like a big step backwards for a band with major hits, but it really wasn't. The malls of America were where the teens shopped, where they hung out, worked, and sometimes played. That a band who could fill a big concert hall would go to places like that, to meet and play for their fans, was an unprecedented gesture, and one which was greatly appreciated by those who already loved them. The whole thing was sponsored by *YM* magazine and Fetish cosmetics—both of which were very popular with teenage girls. Hooking up in that way made sense to everybody.

Again, it made the band *real*. It showed they were regular guys you could get up close and personal with, not just idols you could only see with binoculars in some giant dome. The more of this they did, the better—and longer—the relationship between band and fans would be.

There was, of course, one ideal way to reach millions of people at one time, and that was television. They boys were all over that idea, too. During August, as well as popping up all over the country, they were also on *The Tonight Show with Jay Leno* and *Live! With Regis & Kathie Lee*, pretty much covering both ends of the spectrum. It gave them the adult and family audiences, the late night and the daytime watchers, and gave more people in America the chance to see them than they'd ever had before. Both appearances were landmarks for the boys, their first real appearances on the big three TV networks.

August was the busiest month they'd had in America. There was no chance to go home and relax, even for a couple of days. One thing they'd determined to do, right from the beginning, was to give something back to people. And now they were known, the best way to do that was to take part in concerts where the money would go to good causes. That had happened with the Z100 show, of course, but now they headed into more of them, the first being an event called The Truth Train, in Florida, which had been organized by Students Working Against Tobacco—SWAT—a group that wanted to stop teen smoking. As non-smokers themselves, the boys in 'N Sync were happy to help out, and signed on to appear.

It was a big show, and the band found themselves teamed with some heavy-hitting R&B artists, including Montell Jordan and Liquid Vinyl down in Orlando. It was, however, 'N Sync who were topping the bill, quite a coup against the big names—even if they were on their home turf. Still, it didn't matter who went on first, or who closed the show. It was about the cause, and raising plenty of awareness about the dangers of tobacco.

From there it was directly off to the airport, which they probably knew as well as their houses by now, to catch a flight to California, where they were due to appear the next day. It was another fun-raising event, this organized by KIIS-FM in Los Angeles. The station did this every year, bringing in Top Forty bands to entertain in their "Wango Tango" benefit, with the money being distributed to a host of local charities.

"We played in a stadium and it was a huge rush to be on that stage in front of that many people. There was a good vibe because it was for a good cause, too, so we enjoyed it," JC said.

"It was a lot of fun and it was for a good cause," Chris agreed. "We were really tired. We just did a show last night in Orlando and we had to fly here at like four this morning, so we were beat when we got off the plane. But, you know, when it's for a good cause, and the crowd gets you hyped up it always makes it so much easier."

August had more days left, however, and each of them was filled with things for 'N Sync to do. The next event on their calendar was singing at the Miss Teen Pageant USA, which was something they all enjoyed.

"I fell in love fifty-one times today," Lance joked during the rehearsal. And, when the show aired on CBS, it was easy to see how he could say that. Five extra-cute boys were surrounded by lots and lots of absolute babes. The band sang "I Want You Back" and "God Must Have Spent a Little More Time on You"—maybe the best place they could have found to sing that particular song.

The month culminated in New York, with the opening of the new Virgin Megastore in Union Square. The boys flew in from Atlanta, where they'd been appearing at Macy's the day before, reaching their Manhattan hotel at one A.M. At five they were up again, getting dressed, showered, and breakfasted before meeting in the lobby.

Even at 6:30 in the morning, there were still fans waiting for them, as they hopped into limos headed for the Megastore, where they boarded the open-top double-decker bus that would drive them all over New York city. Richard Bramson, the head of Virgin, was waiting for them, and with him was Petula Clark, the British singer who'd scored such a huge hit with "Downtown" in the

Sixties. She teamed up with the band, and they learned each other's songs to serenade all the passers-by as they drove.

For two and a half hours they went all over the island of Manhattan. With his new look of dark and blond corn-rows (which he'd had done the week before in Orlando, after finding a hairdresser who specialized in braids), Chris was almost unrecognizable at first. Everyone sang a capella.

"I'm used to riding on a bus, just not one without a top," Justin laughed.

Coming back to the store they were greeted by the sight of hundreds of fans gathered and waiting for them, and the boys (with Petula) treated them to a final version of "I Want You Back" before returning to their hotel for lunch. Two hours later they were back at the Mega-store. Their album was playing loudly on the stereo, fill-ing the store. Girls were lined up down the block, anxious to meet the boys and get their autographs.

At one-thirty, the boys entered the store, and pande-monium began as girls rushed forward to meet them. But they were going to be there for a while—an hour and a half to be exact—leaving plenty of time to meet every-body, and also amass a pile of gifts from their fans.

By four o'clock, they were on Broadway again, this time at the MTV studios, where they were taping the *Artist's Cut* show for an hour, before heading off to eat.

Their day wasn't over, however. After a meal, it was off to a radio station, to put in a promo appearance for a couple of hours, talking to listeners, answering questions, and spinning some records. Finally, at nine P.M. they could head back to the hotel. But they didn't have the luxury of sleeping late the next morning. There would be an appearance at the Macy's in New York—the last show of their mini-Macy's tour— then back to Florida, where they were about to begin work on some new recording.

But there would be one brief break, for a little fun. In

September, all the guys got together on a basketball court again. Not for a video this time, but to take part in the annual MTV event, *Rock 'N' Jock Presents: The Game*. It was celebrity hoops, all the proceeds going to charity. As a five-piece, the boys were able to field an entire team, dressed in light blue jerseys (which had to have been Justin's idea). It was fun, a great laugh, and then it was back to work on the album.

BRINGING IT ALL BACK HOME

Unlike their first album, virtually all of their second album would be recorded at their home base, Trans Continental Studios in Orlando. The backing tracks had already been assembled and recorded here and there—Uniontown, Pennsylvania, Frankfurt, Germany, Bronxville, New York, Los Angeles—wherever the various producers were comfortable working.

So why weren't the boys traveling to the producers this time? Mostly, it was nothing more than a matter of time. This album had been on the drawing board for several months, but there'd been literally no block of time when the boys could get into a studio to record before now. It was already September, and the disc was due out in November. That meant they had a total of two weeks in which to record the vocals to fourteen songs—in other words, they had to complete one track a day, which was a lot harder than it sounded.

As soon as the two weeks were up, 'N Sync had major commitments—opening for Janet Jackson on several dates of her tour, then hitting the road as headliners themselves, playing big arenas across the country—and so there'd be no chance to fix any mistakes. They were under the gun. There was no choice but to work as complete professionals.

It helped that many of the songs were already familiar. This was going to be a Christmas album, so some of the songs were standards and traditional pieces, mixed in with the new material. It would have been impossible for any of the guys not to have been familiar with "The First Noël," "O Holy Night," or the Mel Torme tune, "The Christmas Song (Chestnuts Roasting on an Open Fire)."

It was probably fair to wonder just why they were recording a Christmas record when they could have been in the studio laying down completely new material. Christmas records were fine at Christmas, then they were usually put away on the shelf for another eleven months, once December 25 had passed.

There are a couple of answers. Yes, perhaps the album is just seasonal, forgotten for most of the year. But in the time it is played, it brings a lot of joy. More than that, it's played year after year after year, until it becomes something of a tradition in its own right. So, instead of recording something just for the holidays, they were actually creating something that could become timeless.

And Christmas was a special time for all of them, to be with families, wherever possible, and reflect on the joy and love around them. The fact that they were all religious also counted for a lot. In the CD liner notes to *Home For Christmas*, each of the guys offers his thanks to God or to Jesus for the blessings they've enjoyed. It's more than just another commercial venture, it's something heartfelt and honest, true songs of praise.

It was certainly just as well that all the guys really were professional and used to working together, given the time crunch they were under. Between rehearsals and takes, each of the fourteen days proved to be *very* long and tiring, and the knowledge that there'd be no rest at the end of this project had to make them all feel exhausted.

Home For Christmas started off with the title track, a composition by Gary Haase and Rozz Moorhead, with the production and arrangement by John Poppo (Danny Madden was responsible for the sublime co-production on the vocals). The instrumental tracks had been laid down at Quad, in New York, before Poppo had come to Florida to track the boys, and fill out the vocals with the sound of the PM All Star Choir. The song started out hymn-like, with sleigh bells in the background for the Christmas feel before turning to an R&B feel. It evoked the feel of Boyz II Men, one of the big influences on 'N Sync. The harmonies on the bridge and the choruses were nothing short of perfect, subtly filling out Justin's lead, and after the key change, the choir added their voices to the backing. Really, it showcased what the boys did best, which was sing harmony around each other. And it stayed true to what they'd wanted to do, which was bring more of an R&B feel to their music—even moving toward gospel on the fade-out.

"Under My Tree" was a Veit Renn production (he'd done so well by the guys on the *'N Sync* album), and continued that downbeat R&B feeling that just made you want to snuggle in front of a roaring fire, holding someone very special. Written by Shelley Peiken and Guy Roche, it gave the guys a chance to do some real close-harmony work all the way through. The sleigh bells worked their magic again—and there was one stunning moment when the voices cascaded like bells. It was pure romance, innocent and right for the time of year—about the only thing missing was a complimentary sprig of mistletoe. Obviously, they'd all spent a lot of time listening to the modern R&B masters. Sure, it helped that they all had excellent voices that worked superbly together, and there was good material to work with, but they'd come a long way from *'N Sync* and developed their own sound.

Third up came "I Never Knew the Meaning of Christmas," written by producers Evan Rogers and Carl Sturken, and dealing with what Christmas should really be about—and that wasn't what you found in your stocking on Christmas morning. The instrumental tracks to this one had been made in Bronxville, New York, and Los Angeles, before 'N Sync had a chance to sprinkle their own special brand of wonderful on top of it. In style it owed a lot to the work of Babyface, but there was absolutely nothing wrong with that. It was a love song (and there was nothing wrong with that, either), the beats subtle behind the vocals, a gorgeous ballad, with a guitar line that wove in and out of the lead vocal, the full harmonies coming in on the chorus.

"Merry Christmas, Happy Holidays" saw Veit Renn at the controls again. This, however, was a song that particularly stood out for all the guys, since it was co-written by Venn, JC, and Justin, making it extra-personal. Filling out the vocal lines were the Voices of Praise, a choir from the Macedonia Church in Eatonville, Florida. This was more up-tempo, the beats stronger, the first real turn toward pop music. But even then, it could still have been called an R&B song. The chorus showed just how well the boys could blend their voices (including a neat little homage to the Bee Gees in the arrangement of the vocals), and plenty of thought had gone into the arrangement of the harmonies and backgrounds. And, after reaching a climax, the choir came in for a full-on gospel effect that really worked within the song's framework. Superbly catchy, it should have been a single—it would probably have gone straight to Number One over the holidays.

"The Christmas Song (Chestnuts Roasting on an Open Fire)" had been around since the Fifties, co-written by the great jazz singer Mel Torme and Robert Wells. Over the years it had become a standard for the season, covered many times, but never quite like this. The arrangement, and the production, was courtesy of Gary Carolla, who'd recorded the instrumental tracks at his Get Wild Studio, in Uniontown, Pennsylvania, before coming down to Orlando to capture the boys' vocals. The harmonies dated back to the time of the Four Freshmen, and some of the doo-wop bands, but with a soft, jazzy touch, providing the soft cushion for JC's lead voice. Very subtly, they'd updated the song, never losing the warm feel of the original, but making it seem quite right in the context of an R&B record.

"I Guess It's Christmas Time" was another Shelley Peiken song, this time co-written by Peter S. Bliss. Once more Gary Carolla handled the production, bringing the backing tracks down to Trans Continental for the guys to add their vocals. Chris got the chance to show his falsetto abilities on the verse over piano arpeggios, before everyone came in on full harmonies behind him on the ballad. The second verse brought Joey in to sing with Chris, giving a sense of how great it must have sounded the first time they sang together. In some ways, this big ballad, with horns, was a bit out of place, more Celine Dion than Shai, but the guys still did a great job on it.

Veit Renn, who seemed to pull outstanding performances from each of the guys, was behind the board for the Martin Briley/Dana Calitri song "All I Want is You this Christmas." A snaking soprano sax line brought a short introduction straight into the vocal that was melodic over a soft groove, the perfect kind of jam. It emphasized that R&B was the style that seemed to fit the band best these days. Give them the right groove and they could work wonders with their voices, supporting and complementing each other, trading off verses, leads and harmonies. It was beautifully romantic, the kind of song that should only be shared with someone special.

"The First Noel" was the traditional Christmas carol, produced by Gary Carolla again, who also contributed the arrangement. And while it was unusual to hear a carol with beats in the background, the simple fact was that it *worked*, and that was what mattered. The choruses were filled with absolutely glorious harmonies while the boys got to work out a little on the verses. It might have seemed a little weird to the boys, singing all these Christmas songs in the September Florida sunshine and heat, but you'd never have known it from their delivery.

"In Love on Christmas" teamed them with Veit Renn again, opening with very seasonal lines about jingle bells, before breaking into a slow jam with a low, growling bass behind an acoustic guitar. It was the type of song that would have suited Boys II Men, and territory that 'N Sync were rapidly staking out as their own. Being in love at Christmas is always special, and this celebration of that showed just how special the holidays can be. The vocal arrangement was probably the most intricate they'd yet done, harmonies sliding in and out, restrained yet still very emotional.

Gary Carolla was back for "It's Christmas," working alongside Peter Ries. This was the only track where the recording happened in Florida and also Frankfurt, Germany. Opening with the sound of wind and footsteps crunching through the snow, a string ensemble supported the guys' voices on the ballad, which was lovely, but perhaps didn't do them the fullest justice compared to some of the other tracks on the album. Again, it was more Bee Gees than Shai—not a bad thing in itself, by any means, but it seemed as if 'N Sync had moved a little beyond that now. And the song, by Peter Ries and Cherie C. Thomas, seemed a little anonymous in comparison, say, to "Home for Christmas." One quality it definitely did have, shared by all the other songs on the album, was the fact that it was melodious—and it gave the boys a chance to make their own Christmas greetings.

Just how far they'd progressed, and what they could do with their voices, became quite apparent on "O Holy Night," working from Robin Wiley's arrangement on another traditional song. Wiley also produced the track and gave plenty of space to the harmonies. So much work together had made them able to take each other's parts (with the exception of Lance, who was inimitable on the bassline), and blend as if they were brothers, rather than friends who'd come together. It was a daring arrangement, stopping and starting, then harmonies opening like flowers behind the lead. Certainly, no one could listen to this and say these guys couldn't sing—they were up there with any harmony group in the history of music. And so what if it was showing off a little bit? These guys could handle it beautifully, and they'd acquired this special skill. Why not let people see what they could do?

"Love's in Our Hearts on Christmas Day" was yet another song with Veit Renn behind the boards. Another ballad (well, a Christmas record was never going to be an out-and-out dance album, was it?), it used softly swelling strings behind the verses. It wasn't until the second verse that the harmonies appeared behind the lead voice. This was really a standout track, in large part because of the R&B feel the writers had given it, even with the string arrangement, which at times was almost baroque, particularly on the bridge. The first time around, it sounded a little strange, but then, once you were used to it, it became one of the coolest songs on the entire record.

Veit Renn was basically all over this album, and since he worked magic with the guys, that wasn't a bad thing. He was also the producer of "The Only Gift," written by Maria Christensen and Jeff Franzell. It started like a ballad, but quickly became a lovely Christmassy slow jam. Unlike the previous song, this really utilized the boys' harmonies, their strongest suit. Even Lance got a little lead at the end of the second verse, leading into the chorus. And putting in a quote from "Deck the Halls" was positively inspired!

Since Renn had done so much on the album, it was only fitting that the last track should also belong to him, in more ways than one. He not only produced "Kiss Me at Midnight," he also co-wrote it, along with Kenny Lamb. And a stronger way to end a holiday record could hardly be imagined. With the countdown, it evoked New Year's Eve. Now *this* was a dance track, still seasonal, but with one of the most infectious choruses in recent memory (maybe even more than "I Want You Back"). And there was a very cool Seventies funk midsection on the synthesizer, all resolving itself with a key change that didn't even stretch the guys' vocal cords, the chorus repeating through the fade, until it couldn't have been more attached to a listener if it had used fish hooks.

All told, it was an absolute triumph. To cynics, a Christmas album might have seemed like an exercise in exploitation, but the boys had made it into something very worthwhile, one of the best new Christmas albums in years. They could have played it safe and covered hymns, carols, and standards. Instead, they'd shown the direction they'd be taking in the future, leaning much more toward R&B, which really suited their voices best. Given the right song and arrangement (of which there were plenty here), there was no one better than them around. And after this no one would be calling them BSB clones again. They'd proved—even though it was never in doubt—that they were a band of real substance and talent, who were going to be around for a long time to come.

CHRISTMAS CAME EARLY

The album was the perfect prelude to their own headlining tour. Everyone had high hopes for it, but probably no one expected what happened—that it would crash into the *Billboard* album charts at number seven! *'N Sync* was already up there, hovering at number four, with three million copies sold, in November. For any band to have two albums in the Top Ten was almost unheard of, certainly since the glory days of the Beatles or Elvis Presley. Certainly no one could say that the boys hadn't arrived now—and in fine style, too.

As 1998 closed, *Home For Christmas* remained in the Top Ten, having very quickly gone platinum, with more than a million copies sold, a remarkable feat for a Christmas album in its first year. *'N Sync* was at number three, still selling like hotcakes, having now passed the *four* million mark.

And that wasn't all. Although the guys didn't officially have a single out, there was enough radio play for "God Must Have Spent a Little More Time on You" to propel it to number thirty-four in the singles chart. If they'd chosen to put it out on its own, there was no doubt it would have been a total smash.

All in all, it was the perfect way to end an amazing year, at least in terms of sales. Throughout the industry there'd been talk of a lot of proven artists not performing well. A new Whitney Houston album hadn't sold anywhere near as well as had been hoped. Hanson's new live record had sold disappointingly, barely going gold. Even Mariah Carey's hit collection hadn't zoomed to the top. What 1998 had been, really, was a year for teen bands. Matchbox 20 had sold seven million copies of their debut album. The Backstreet Boys were still up there with their album. Brandy had done amazingly well, both as a singles and album artist. And 'N Sync had defied all expectations by having two albums in the top ten.

The guys had come home, after all their success abroad, and just stomped all over the American charts. The time had finally been right for pop music, and more specifically, boy bands in the U.S., and 'N Sync had been at the forefront. They'd shown themselves with the single, then the album, and consolidated it all with the Christmas record. Others, like 98 Degrees and Five, were following in their wake, but delivering the goods wasn't going to be easy now—'N Sync had raised the bar for all the others. They'd even won their first awards, two *Billboard* Music Video awards for "I Want You Back" which had been voted Best Clip of the Year and Best New Artist Clip of the Year in the dance video category.

In some ways they'd even become more successful than their supposed rivals, BSB (although, in real life, there was absolutely no animosity between them; the two bands had hardly even seen each other, since they were both so busy). There was only one thing left for the guys to do, which would really consolidate their position, and that was to undertake a headlining tour of America. Playing stadiums and arenas—and selling them out—would be the final, ultimate proof that they'd arrived.

The tour, which would last more than two months, would take them all across the United States, starting in Orlando on November 18, through the South, East Coast, and Midwest, before taking a two-week Christmas break from the thirteenth to the twenty-seventh of December. It would pick up again in Minneapolis, the site of their first triumph (although not the Mall of America this time; instead, they'd be playing the Orpheum), then heading west and southwest during January. Then there'd be a break until the end of February, when the guys would use their free time to record their new album, before hitting the road gain through March and April, covering all the remaining cities of the U.S. It was, all things considered, one of the biggest and longest American tours anyone had undertaken in recent memory.

Before it all began, though, there'd be another rerun of their *In Concert* special for the Disney Channel on November 11, followed on December 5 by *Holiday In Concert*, where they'd feature songs from the *Home For Christmas* album. The show was scheduled to be repeated several times between its first airing and Christmas Day.

That was only part of their television commitment, however. November 13 would bring an appearance on the *Ricki Lake Show*. Even their Christmas vacation wasn't completely free of appearances. December 15 saw them return to *Live! With Regis and Kathie Lee*. The following day had them on twice, first bright and early with *CBS This Morning*, and then later with *Kathie Lee Christmas*, also for CBS. Their television exposure would actually hit a peak on Christmas Day itself, as they took part in *Walt Disney World's Very Merry Christmas Parade* on ABC.

Throughout the country, tickets for their shows were selling like crazy, and venues were putting up the SOLD OUT signs. The two-week break, in as much as it was a break at all, was necessary. It did give the guys a chance to spend time with their families over the holiday, although the day after Christmas would see them boarding a plane and heading north. More importantly, it gave them a brief rest from a very grueling schedule. The first month of the tour would only give them seven nights off, not much when you consider all the traveling and the constant strain of performances, both on bodies and voices. The second leg was slightly easier, but still wearing, with longer distances between shows, and so more time actually on the road. But when they got out on the stage and heard all the fans screaming, they knew that this was what it was all about, this was why they were pushing themselves so hard.

Did it seem right for them to concentrate so much on America at the expense of the fans in other parts of the world who'd first supported them? Perhaps, but the truth was that later in 1999 they'd be getting their own chance to see the guys after the new record was out everywhere. It was going to be a very long year for the guys, one which would see them having very little down time in which to relax.

Certainly it all got off to a very good start. On the first *Billboard* chart of the year, *'N Sync* rose one place to the number two slot, held off the top position by Garth Brooks's double live album, which had sold a record-breaking twelve million copies in just five weeks. *Home For Christmas* dropped to number ten, but that was probably only to be expected, given that Christmas had passed. The video of "Merry Christmas, Happy Holidays" had seen quite a bit of airplay on the music video channels over the season, and next November it was certain that the record would be in the stores again, something of a perennial, back year after year, and bound to sell consistently well.

'N Sync had laid all the foundations for their success quite solidly, and now they were in the position to reap the rewards. They still rehearsed in the Orlando warehouse where the temperature could sometimes climb into the nineties. But it would be a few months before they'd have to work out some new routines. For now, their show was set, and they'd be doing it for the fans night after night after night, for well over sixty U.S. dates.

They'd come a long, long way in a relatively short time, considering that three years before they didn't even have a record deal, let alone their first hit. But they'd caught the moment, they were doing something very right. They'd built up a lot of momentum, and now they were riding it, which was all they could do. People loved them; you only had to look at album sales, the way concert tickets had all been snapped up, and the other things—calendars, posters, T-shirts—to understand how massive, and how global they'd become. Web sites dedicated to them had proliferated. There was really no telling where it would all end.

Over Christmas 1998, each of the guys had a chance to reflect on everything that had happened, and understand that the chemistry had been perfect when they all came together. That was something that happened rarely. Sure, they had some disagreements when they were out on the road. Spending so much time together in a small space, that was inevitable. But behind it all was a love for each other, an understanding and forgiveness. They could laugh at one another and at themselves, taking each day as something new, a fresh start to be enjoyed. They'd come a long way in one another's company, and there was still a long, long way to go. And where it might end is anyone's guess.

KICKIN' IT

The story of 'N Sync's rise to the top—and make no mistake, they really have reached the top—is a testament to talent and persistence. To succeed, you have to have faith in your own abilities, to be confident (which isn't the same as being cocky or over-confident), and you have to be willing to work hard—very hard—with the desire to make it.

Those are the qualities all the boys have always shown. Whether it was Chris singing for tips in coffee shops or Justin strutting his stuff on *Star Search*, the desire to succeed has always been inside them, and they've all kept pushing. Of course, the fact is that they all happen to be very good singers and dancers with tremendous natural ability. While they wanted to do well, as Chris said, "We don't look at trying to be the top group. We just want to be a good group." And no one can deny they've managed that. The key, as Justin pointed out, is "practice, practice, practice. Always practice your craft to be the best you can be. It takes dedication and a little bit of luck."

Sure, things have become very strange for the guys,

and they find themselves in situations where "people come up to you and know everything and you've never even seen them before." They've become public property. But, along the way, they've achieved the most "gratifying" thing—real success and acclaim at home. Being in Florida and telling people they were big in Europe or big in Asia was one thing. Being able to point to the charts and see their single or their album was another thing altogether. It proved something to everyone, and made things complete for the guys.

The work they put in when nobody knew them, and no one, beyond their families, cared, has paid off in a big way. Long, late hours in hot rooms, sweating through the routines they'd devised and worked out for themselves, writing songs and filling in harmonies. They did it back then because they loved music and dancing, and they felt that together they could contribute something, offer audiences something different. In those days, if they talked about international fame, it was more as a joke than anything. What's happened has gone way beyond all their wildest dreams. If you'd told the guys in the fall of 1995 that they wouldn't be able to walk down a street anywhere in the world without being mobbed, they'd have said you were nuts. But dreams do come true. They built it all up slowly and sensibly, one step at a time, thanks to some very savvy management and handling by Lou Pearlman and Johnny Wright. Germany was the foundation for 'N Sync, and the rest of their success has been built on that.

Being cute is a huge plus (and let's face it, is anyone going to pay to watch someone ugly?), and the boys *are* all really cute. But beauty is only skin deep, as the saying goes. Talent goes all the way to the bone.

The band's climb to the top might have seemed pretty easy, and, compared to many others, it has been quite straightforward. But along the way, they've logged thousands of miles, sung thousands of times, gone without sleep, performed when they've been sick or just weary, and given their all every time. The fans have believed in them because they've believed in their fans.

Justin, Chris, Joey, Lance, and JC aren't just some faces and bods on a stage or on a video. They're real people, very human, and they've always taken the time to make sure people know that. They remember what it's like to look up to others—they still do it themselves—and that things are so much better if you know who that person is. Okay, so it gets out of hand at times, maybe when the fans come from all over to look at their houses and things like that, but it goes with the territory, and they accept that. Without the fans, they don't have a career.

Being stars is about much more than fame and fortune. It's also about responsibility. If people are looking up to them, then the guys feel they have to be good role models. They don't drink, they don't smoke, they don't do drugs. They're very positive people. Not only do they owe it to themselves to keep their bodies in top shape, they owe it to the people who are buying their records and coming to see them. Spiritual values are important to them. They follow their faith—but at the same time, they're not going to push it at anyone else. Beliefs are a choice, made personally.

They're clean, they're wholesome. Some cynics would say they're too good to be true, but that would be just jealousy talking. The bottom line is that these guys are professionals. Four of them had made their livings as entertainers—even Justin, although he was still in school—before the band even started. And Lance, the only one who hadn't been a professional, was already a veteran. And being a professional means taking care of your instrument. For a singer and dancer, that's the body. It's as simple as that, really. To do what they do, the acrobatic dance routines, the guys have to be in the best possible shape, on top of things all the time.

* * *

So, where can they go from here? When you're already at the top, what exactly can you do? The answer, at least on the evidence of *Home For Christmas*, is that they boys are going to really explore their R&B side. That they have the ability to do it is beyond question. Their voices are as soulful as any. And it makes sense, since bands like Boys II Men and Shai were fairly direct inspirations for their overall sound. One thing they'll definitely never lose is a sense of melody. It's there in every song on both their albums, one of the band's defining factors.

While they haven't done too much songwriting so far—at least, not much of it has appeared on record— that will probably change. Now they're more used to the studio and to the business, they'll be able to approach things with greater confidence.

"We collaborate on everything," Justin said. "I think we have our influence on everything we do, not just the dancing, but also on the music. If we don't like the song, our producers won't make us do it. We've had chances to come up with our own harmonies, and things like that."

Those contributions will only get bigger as time passes. The guys are all fast learners (they have to be, really), and they've discovered what works and what doesn't. They're also discovering more about themselves as they grow, new abilities they never even realized they had. It's not impossible that a few years down the road there could be an 'N Sync album that's written, sung, played, and produced by the guys. And you can't get any more self-contained than that!

Whether they go that particular route or not, it's safe to say that the boys will only become more soulful as they get older. Not that they'll ignore dance tunes—how could they, when they love to dance themselves? But the slow jams are something they can really get into, where the harmonies can shine, and the harmonies are what help make them so very special.

There'll be more tours, even bigger tours, and a new record in the not-too-distant future to help keep the fans happy. About the only things the guys won't get is rest. Their calendars are already booked solid well into the year 2000.

Entertaining the world is a big job, but Chris, Joey, Justin, JC, and Lance are more than up to the task. They've torn up the charts and the record books, they've established themselves as massive. Everybody loves them, and the future is all theirs. Rarely have five boys been so much in sync, vocally or personally. And rarely have the fans responded so positively to a sound. Maybe it's just the right time and the right place. Maybe, just maybe, the whole world is 'n sync. It certainly seems that way.

'N SYNC ON THE NET

So you've got the 'puter, you've got the modem, and you've got the Internet connection. Cool. Take a little time and do some checking on some of the top sites on the boys. There are over one hundred sites already, but these are the very best.

The first place to point your web browser, obviously, is the official 'N Sync site, which will keep you up to date on all the news, concert dates, what's coming up for record release—you'll know it all before anyone else. Just go to *www.nsync.com* and you'll have it all happening.

A lot of people use America Online for their service, so it's only right that AOL should have a lot of 'N Sync material on their site. If you use them, type in the keyword NSYNC and you'll find everything they have to offer. The boys have also done chats on Yahoo. If you go to *www.yahoo.com* and type 'N Sync, you'll probably be able to find the transcripts

'N Sync Town would be a pretty cool place to live. You can't quite do that, but you can visit, at *www.geocities.com/SunsetStrip/Stadium/2159.*

There's two whole 'N Sync worlds where you can lose yourself. Find one at *www.angelfire.com/fl/bankh*, and the other at *www.members.tripod.com/~nsyncplanet*.

Maybe the best-named site is God Must Have Spent a Little More Time on 'N Sync, and the creators certainly spent plenty of time on putting it together. Check it out at *www.geocities.com/SunsetStrip/Frontrow/3530*.

This site's webmistress seems to be majorly crushing on Lance, but she gives plenty of room to the other guys too. Check it out at *www.angelfire.com/il/laurennlance/index.html*.

To go to 'N Sync Heaven, click on *www.geocities.com/SunsetStrip/Studio/9143/*.

And, finally, there's the 'N Sync Unofficial Site, which you can reach at *www.nunsync.com/*.

For more addresses—and there are plenty of them—just type 'N Sync in your favorite search engine, and you'll be there before you know it. Basically, anything you want to know about any of the guys, including a ton of pictures, some interviews, news (and did I mention a lot of pictures?), you can find by going through the Web sites. Have fun.

If you don't have a computer, you can still get hold of the boys. The 'N Sync Fan Club can be found at P.O. Box 692109, Orlando FL 32869-2109.

DISCOGRAPHY VIDEOGRAPHY

'N Sync *(All except America)*

Tearin' Up My Heart/ Riddle/ Here We Go/ For the Girl Who Has Everything/ Best of My Life/ You Got It/ I Need Love/ I Want You Back/ More Than a Feeling/ Together Again/ Crazy for You/ Sailing/ Forever Young/ Giddy Up

'N Sync *(American Version)*

Tearin' Up My Heart/ I Jusy Wanna Be with You/ Here We Go/ For the Girl Who Has Everything/ God Must Have Spent a Little More Time on You/ You Got It/ I Need Love/ I Want You Back/ Everything I Own/ I Drive Myself Crazy/ Crazy for You/ Sailing/ Giddy Up

Home For Christmas

Home for Christmas/ Under My Tree/ I Never Knew the Meaning of Christmas/ Merry Christmas, Happy

Holidays/ The Christmas Song (Chestnuts Roasting on an Open Fire)/ I Guess it's Christmas Time/ All I Want is You This Christmas/ The First Noel/ In Love on Christmas/ It's Christmas/ O Holy Night (A Capella)/ Love's in Our Hearts on Christmas Day/ The Only Gift/ Kiss Me at Midnight

In The Mix: The Official Home Video

I Want You Back (U.S. and European video)
Tearin' Up My Heart
For the Girl Who Has Everything
Here We Go
God Must Have Spent a Little More Time on You
Merry Christmas, Happy Holidays
(also live footage of "Tearin' Up My Heart," "I Want You Back," "Crazy For You," as well as interviews with the guys)